T0065178

BIRTHING PURPOSE OUT OF PAIN

From Pain to Purpose

AUTHOR LOVE

authorHOUSE®

AuthorHouse™
1663 Liberty Drive
Bloomington, IN 47403
www.authorhouse.com
Phone: 833-262-8899

Published by AuthorHouse 09/12/2023

ISBN: 978-1-6655-6835-7 (sc)
ISBN: 978-1-6655-6836-4 (e)

Print information available on the last page.

Any people depicted in stock imagery provided by Getty Images are models, and such images are being used for illustrative purposes only. Certain stock imagery © Getty Images.

This book is printed on acid-free paper.

Because of the dynamic nature of the Internet, any web addresses or links contained in this book may have changed since publication and may no longer be valid. The views expressed in this work are solely those of the author and do not necessarily reflect the views of the publisher, and the publisher hereby disclaims any responsibility for them.

CONTENTS

INTRODUCTION

I remember the day God changed the title of my book. While in prayer and consecration, he gave me a word concerning his powerful plan for my book. I was sitting on the couch one day when the Lord spoke to me, "Birthing Purpose Out of Pain." I then said, "Thank you God!" I had been praying specific prayers during this writing process. I wanted my memoir to be Holy Spirit led and inspired. Prior to writing this book, I also received a word to revisit and re-edit my book because I was going to find healing through writing this memoir. This word came through a midnight cry one night, and God's word does not return to him void according to Isaiah 55:11! This was the first step to my healing! I am healing healthy, and I love it!

Before going on my healing journey, pain was like love to me. My past experiences contradicted what healthy love is. I did not know how to differentiate the two. My biggest battle was the battle that was going on in my head. My mind was a battlefield daily. Some days, I did not feel like getting out of bed. I felt stuck and unable to move forward from some of the wrong decisions I had made in the past. Some of my decisions were coming from a place of brokenness, until I realized that I needed to get to the root of the problem. I started to unpack my trauma layer by layer. This was the most painful part of my healing journey.

I am grateful that I have had such amazing women that have played compelling roles in my life. They reminded me that there is hope for me and my pain doesn't determine who God created me to be. I didn't have to struggle alone anymore, closed in and afraid of allowing myself to be vulnerable about my truths and past experiences. These women poured into me, prayed for me, and labored with me while on my healing journey.

My mother is a woman of faith and prayer who is truly anchored in the word of God. She continues to pray over all of her children and grandchildren, even to this day. I know her prayers have helped me while God intervened on my behalf. I no longer internalize pain because I am now free from the bondage of past trauma.

I don't look like what I've been through. I was once broken and lost, but God has restored me and forgiven me for my transgressions. Only God gets the glory out of my life!

I've learned that pain produces power. In the midst of my trials, God allowed me to know my purpose and to find strength in Christ Jesus. In my weakness, God was made strong, and I was able to persevere through life's trials. I realized that there was purpose in the rejection, betrayal, disappointments, depression, sexual and physical abuse, abandonment, and betrayal, and all glory belongs to God! The Bible teaches in Revelation 12:11 (KJV), "And they overcame him by the blood of the Lamb, and by the word of their testimony…"

I am an overcomer! The pain has positioned me for the calling that was placed on my life. During warfare, God put the right connections in my life that gave me warfare strategies and taught me how to defeat the enemy with the word of God, prayer and action. God has shown me that my discernment is active and heightened. I now realize that I am an atmosphere changer. I am able to walk into an atmosphere, feel the heaviness in that atmosphere and change it, even if I go into a witchcraft atmosphere that is not of God.

For many years I didn't know my identity in Christ Jesus, but God has given me clarity and confirmation of my God-given-purpose. I realize that a lot of the mixed emotions I had was because I allowed people to mislabel who I was in God, until God gave me clarity and I learned to depend on the word of God. Once I acknowledged that Jesus is the only Lord, I was converted. My life changed and my mindset was shifted. Everything around me began to align with the plans of God. I was never the same.

My life story is actually like a woman who is pregnant and going through the process of pain, contractions and much more. After carrying a baby for 9 months, on that due date is when the pushing has to take place. New life has to spring forth! I knew that it was my pushing time. In the pregnancy is where the molding, shaping, endurance, and suffering take place. However, I had been pregnant way too long, and I knew that it was my time to push out the promise, word, and divine purpose. God told me, "Now is the time to come forth, daughter! This is your birthing season!"

And the God of all grace, who called you to his eternal glory in Christ, after you have suffered a little while, will himself restore you and make you strong, firm and steadfast. (1 Peter. 5:10, NIV)

I now know that my trials weren't in vain. Spending time with God showed me that I was stuck in childhood trauma, and had given too many people access to me. What I experienced from my childhood to teenage years caused me to have a mental illness called severe depression. Starting at the age of 5 years old, I became a broken little girl who eventually grew into a broken woman, not realizing how important it was to deal with those painful wounds. I understood that being saved was good, but I needed more. So, God provided me with the necessary strategies, resources, and people to help me during my healing journey. As his daughter, God showed me that perishing was not an option, but healing was my portion. God is so faithful!

ACKNOWLEDGEMENTS

First of all, I want to give glory to God for inspiring me to write this powerful memoir. I wasn't sure, or didn't feel that I had what it takes to birth this book. In the midst of my insecurities, God told me to do it anyway. I realize that if it wasn't for God allowing me to go through trials, pain, and opposition, I wouldn't have a testimony to tell someone how God got me through it and allowed my trials to push me into my purpose.

I want to give honor to my Lord and savior for using me as a vessel to go through some of life's traumatic experiences, so that I can be a witness of how good God is. I realize that my trials and tribulations are what built my character in God. Telling my life story was uncomfortable because it opened painful and difficult memories of my life. Some things I dealt with, while other parts of my life I swept under the carpet and went on with life as usual. Oftentimes we must get over the stigma that women are to be strong no matter what. Instead, we should always encourage healing and wholeness in Christ.

At the age of 24, I visited a church my male cousin John invited me to, and I received a prophetic word. The visiting minister told me, "God said you've been through so much. God said write a book. Your book is going to bless someone's life. Someone needs to hear your story."

I want to thank God for giving me the confidence to be obedient to write this book. Once afraid and unassured, I was too ashamed to open up about some of my life experiences. Every time I started writing, it seemed like I was not able to finish my book. However, fourteen years later, God said, "Now is the time to finish your book". With discipline and faith, I started writing my book and did not stop until it was completed.

I want to thank God for my mother who has always been there for me and saw the best in me when I did not see my own potential. I realize, as a parent myself, that a mother's love runs deep, but a mother who fears the Lord knows how to come boldly before the throne of grace. My mother was there a lot through my depression, and she always spoke life even when I was suicidal. Sometimes, my mind could not wrap around the fact that my mother sacrificed so much of herself for her children. I oftentimes wonder if she ever took the time to heal from all the pressure and the issues that she had to face as a parent. I am grateful to have a mother that loved me enough to teach me the word of God and how to stand on God's word. My mother planted powerful seeds that helped bless my life. I learned a lot of amazing attributes from my mother. She taught me to have morals and respect myself as a lady. Most importantly, she emphasized that my worth is in God and that man's validation is not necessary. I always struggled in that area, but the older I got, the more I understood what she meant.

I want to thank God for my father. Without him there is no me. Even in the midst of our relationship, I have never stopped loving him and praying for him.

I must honor my Grandma Mrs. Thang. My granny got this name because she was truly a virtuous woman, but she was also a jazzy first lady. She was the matriarch of the family and a virtuous woman who was honored by many because of the God that dwelt within her. She was the one who brought the atmosphere of God no matter where she went. I learned so much from her. I was a grandma's baby. The time that she spent with me while she was here on earth was priceless. My grandma was a pastor and a woman of wisdom and love. She dropped jewels every time I was in her presence. I learned about wife duties, how to cover my husband, and how to budget my finances. My grandmother planted seeds in me that I am forever grateful for. She displayed love and left behind a powerful legacy of love.

I want to honor my favorite aunt Cookie. She was definitely my safe place as a child growing up. She helped shape me into the woman I am now. I admire her strength and passion for her goals. I gained so much support as she helped me navigate through life's journey.

I also want to honor my spiritual mother Rose whom I sat under in ministry for years. This woman of God was a great influence in my life. Her love, laughter, support, and nurturing spirit were priceless. During the difficult moments of my life's journey, she taught and equipped me concerning the things of God.

I must take the time to appreciate the support from my siblings. My little sister Kekee has been there through the roughest times of my journey, watching me struggle with depression, due to childhood trauma. At such a young age, I experienced spiritual warfare before I understood it. Being chosen is not easy at all. Oftentimes, I did not want to be chosen, or carry the oil. As a little sister, I know it was hard for her to witness her big sister deal with the difficulties of life and not be affected. The most powerful blessings of God's plans are what prevailed in my life. My siblings watched me accomplish many milestones in my life. I remember when my sister helped me with my children while working and going to college. I want to also thank God for both of my brothers Lamar and Dale who have been supportive and assisted me with their nieces and nephews while I worked and provided for my children. I love my siblings and thank God for them!

I want to thank God for all my children. My oldest Dontae helped me become a better mother and pushed me to make something out of my life. I am thankful for my son's beautiful fiancé Brooklyn and my bonus daughter who have brought so much love, support, and balance to my son's life. I thank God for my middle daughter Reny and my baby Taylor who has a servant's heart. My youngest daughter is my little intercessor and praise dancer. My family is the reason why I wake up every morning and add pressure and go after my dreams. I carry all my children in my spirit daily, praying for their success and that they will live a purposeful life. I would not be the woman I am without having a supportive family that stands behind me and the village that helps support the family.

I want to also acknowledge my children's father James for all the support that he contributes to me and his children. Even in challenging moments, we work hand in hand to make sure we provide the best life that we possibly can for our children.

I want to thank God for my closest male cousin John. I appreciate the genuine support and love he gives me. I am grateful he plays a major role in my life. He is a humble and meek servant of the Lord. We have a like-minded spirit, and I love him like a biological brother.

I want to acknowledge my mentor, Sharon. I was about 16 years of age when I met this influential woman through a teen pregnancy program called Suma. Instead of allowing me to have a pity party about getting pregnant early, Sharon spoke life into me. I remember the conversation like it was yesterday. "Ok you got pregnant, but what are you going to do about it? This does not have to be the end of your story. This is the beginning of your story. Allow your son to be the reason you don't ever settle again but follow your dreams." That moment I knew I had the responsibility to follow my dreams, not just for me, but I had a child that was depending on me. This woman convinced me at the age of 16 that I could achieve any goal I set my mind to.

I want to appreciate and thank God for my best friend Shay. We practically raised our children together. From disciplining our children to picking them up from daycare, there was never a moment when we were alone as parents because we were always connected as a village. I absolutely love the fact that we were drawn to each other by the Spirit of God. Shay is a woman of faith, and God has done some miraculous things in her life.

I want to thank God for my sister in the Lord and pastor friend Monica. She and I are practically family. We have been great friends since junior high school. She was that friend that knew how to get a prayer in. I love her and always carry her in my spirit. Monica has always been supportive and has a compassionate spirit without judgment.

I thank God for my big spiritual sister Kiesha. I was not really big on meeting new people, but she has spoken into my life and supported every business idea and women empowerment gathering that I have ever had. This woman of God has a spirit of excellence that is contagious, and it gleams off her to people that she encounters. This is an authentic and divine connection, that I know for sure.

I want to give honor where honor is due. I want to acknowledge my great author friend Reree for being like a sister to me, supporting me and encouraging me to write my first book. She is an incredibly loving person and does not mind sharing resources. Reree's goal is that other women thrive in life.

I want to thank God for my sister Trina. She and I go way back. I've known my sis since I was 10 years old. We went to the same school and our families lived in the same neighborhood. Over the years, our friendship has grown into a sisterly bond. I love her like she is my blood sister. She is a powerful woman whom God has used many times to give me a prophetic word in my life, and I've watched God move. I am grateful to know her. She and my cousin have three children together, so now we really are family. We have raised our children around each other since they were in the womb.

I want to acknowledge, also, the Women Connect Ministry. I am the founder of the Women Connect Community on Facebook and Women Connected on Purpose on Instagram. I appreciate every woman that has been supportive of the vision of the Women Connect Ministry that God has given me. I love seeing women rise from broken places and identify their purpose in life and walk in it. I thank God for every woman that has shared her testimony and was a part of any prayer breakfast or luncheon. Thank you ladies! Keep growing!

I want to thank God for my author friend Tammy who is an overseer and whom I love dearly. This woman has supported me in my writing process and introduced me to other authors across the world. The support that I receive from her is amazing. I am so grateful for this divine connection.

I want to acknowledge my marketing coach friend Miya. I met this amazing lady on Facebook. She is an author, motivational speaker, and a marketing strategist coach. God has used this woman to pour into me so many times. I tell you, God will use complete strangers to bless your life. She has definitely been a blessing to my life.

I want to thank my good friend Shelly who is a minister at Cincinnati Public Schools. She invited me to a powerful women empowerment called "Live to Move", and my life was changed from that moment. This ministry has blessed me.

My dear sister in the Lord, Evette, is the CEO of a powerful women's ministry, and she has been such a blessing to me and every woman that is connected to this ministry. I love and thank God for this amazing connection of women that he allowed to cross my path. I remember praying that God would put me in the presence of women who are authentic, who know who they are in God and who are advancing the kingdom.

I want to thank God for my sister Trisha whom I met at CPS. God has truly connected us together as sisters in Christ. I am grateful for the love, prayers, and support that we extend to one another.

I must acknowledge my church family, the Revival Center of Cincinnati for taking myself and my family in after we moved on from a church where our ministry was no longer active. I am grateful that my pastor allows me to teach the teens. I realize that spiritual growth is especially important. I thank God for my pastor, all the elders and deacons, and everyone who makes up the local body.

Giving Thanks

I want to thank God for everyone who has impacted my life, or who was a lesson in my life's journey. Everything serves a purpose. Whether it was good, bad or indifferent, it worked out for my good. I want to thank God for all the friends and Christian coaches that provoked me to be better and to step out on faith and do what God has called me to do. I recall a time when a beautiful kingdom woman told me her powerful testimony of when God told her to do something that was odd and didn't make sense. She said, "Sometimes when God tells you to do something you will look foolish at first, but because he is God, men's approval is not necessary." She obeyed God even when people said that it was not God. She kept showing up anyway until that very thing that God purposed for her life generated wealth like no other and provoked other women to show up and be the best versions of themselves. She was also given a platform to help women find their voices, step out on faith and do what God had called them to do. The bible teaches that we overcome by the blood of the lamb and by the word of our testimony. Her testimony not only helped me, but it has helped many males and females all over the world. She also emphasized how important it is not to tell people your vision, but as God gives it to you, pray over it and ask God to give you provision and strategies.

I am also thankful for the people that did not give up on me while I was in my healing journey. I am still healing, but I am healing healthy with God. I am no longer internalizing those emotions of pain and trauma, but I am allowing God to transform me. God showed me the ones that were making a mockery out of the pain I was enduring, but he would not allow me to curse them. He told me to just pray for them. He also told me that they were not called to my life, but were just seasonal connections. I am grateful for the family and friends that kept me covered as I was going through. I remember God once revealing to me that we as people don't pray and undergird one another while going through, but we should. Galatians 6:1 (ESV) says, "Brothers, if anyone is caught in any transgression, you who are spiritual should restore him in the spirit of gentleness. Keep watch on yourself, lest you too be tempted." I thank God for his grace and mercy when I did not always get it right. God was always there with open arms. God's promise is always yay and amen.

CHAPTER 1

In The Beginning

I WAS BORN JANUARY 26, 1982, IN CINCINNATI, OHIO, TO MY MOTHER Constance and my father Man. My mother was around eighteen years of age and still in high school when she got pregnant with me. After my mother gave birth to me, my grandma Mrs. Thang named me. From the moment my grandma laid eyes on me, she took me under her wing.

My father was not present at the hospital, but my mother's mom and family were present. My mother's life took a different direction when I was born because she was embarking on an unfamiliar journey called motherhood. My mother was so excited to bring her baby girl home. She looked at me and said, "My God! You are so beautiful," as she held me and sniffed my baby scent. My mother was afraid to fail as a mother, so she experienced many emotions at one time.

A couple of days after being released from the hospital, I started having breathing complications. One day while I was at home, I started gasping for air. My mom walked into her bedroom, looked inside my crib, and saw that I was taking shallow breaths. She got scared and called my grandma, and they rushed me to the hospital. Once I got to the hospital, admissions rushed me straight back to the ER. As a nineteen-year-old mother, my mom was afraid because she thought she was going to lose me. She began to cry as my grandmother called for the elders of the church to come to the hospital to pray. Still unable to breathe, I was rushed to the ICU to be put on oxygen. My mom and some of the church leaders were in the waiting room. People gathered around my mother and grandma for moral support. My mother began to get impatient because she had no idea what was happening to her baby girl.

The doctor finally came into the waiting area and told my mother that I had bronchitis, and I was unable to go home because my oxygen level was too low. My mother began to cry again because she did not understand exactly what the disease was. My grandma pulled the doctor to the side and asked, "Doctor, can we go into the ICU to pray?" She expressed, "It's urgent." Usually, only the parents can go into the ICU. But God softened the heart of the doctor. So when my mother, grandmother, and the elders went into the ICU, they gathered around my bed and prayed. The doctors said I was not going to make it because my lungs were too weak, but God had other plans. A powerful prophecy was given to my mother by one of the evangelists at her church. "God says she is going to make it, and she is chosen by God to do a mighty work in the Lord. She will endure many trials, but the Lord will bring her through it all." My mom cried tears of joy because of the prophetic word that was given to her, and at that moment her faith was strengthened.

On the seventh day I was released from the hospital. My mother brought me home and watched me closely. I was prescribed medicine and given paperwork from the doctor explaining my diagnosis and the medicine, which was to keep my bronchitis under control. My mother picked up my medicine and started me on it right away. I was using an asthma pump and a breathing treatment daily while at home to help me breathe better. By the time I started walking, my breathing had improved, but I still had to use inhalers and get breathing treatments.

The powerful prophecy was spoken over my life, and my mother began to meditate on the prophecy. She had feared losing me—her only child at the time–but now she had the reassurance that God had a purpose and plan for my life.

I was a part of a village of strong women. My grandma kept me in church from the time I was a baby. I had every kind of dress in all colors with bows and little bootie shoes. When my mother started going to beauty school, my grandmother watched me.

CHAPTER 2

Childhood

M Y HEALTH WAS A CHALLENGE GROWING UP. MY BRONCHITIS interfered with my physical activities in grade school and at home. I had to keep my asthma pump with me at all times. I even had to keep one at school. One day while playing outside with my mother's friend's daughters, we were climbing trees and playing tag when all of a sudden I started wheezing and couldn't breathe. At the time we lived in the projects in the Fairmount area. I was called into the house to take my inhaler and my breathing treatment, but the medicine did not open up my airways. That same day I was rushed to the hospital, and they kept me overnight. I remember being hospitalized on several occasions. My condition definitely altered my life.

I started school at six years of age because my birthday came late. Because of my medical diagnosis, my mother kept me close to her. So when I started attending kindergarten in the elementary school in my aunt's neighborhood, it was new and scary at the same time. Prior to kindergarten, I did not go to daycare or preschool, so I had to learn how to adapt to being around my peers. School wasn't so bad in the beginning because my favorite cousin, Keyshia, was there, and we were close. However, school changed for me when they sent me to a Catholic school.

One day, in class the teacher walked up to me and said they were going to call my home because I had stolen the school belongings. While the teacher was on the phone with my mother, I started crying and the children began laughing at me. Some students in my class had plotted against me and put playdough and scissors in my bookbag. So, I was blamed for something I did not do. I remember how that made me feel as a child. I was so humiliated. When I got home, my mother started yelling at me.

"Why are you taking things? You have every toy you can name in this house!"

I replied, "Mommy, I did not steal," as tears ran down my cheeks.

For some reason, I knew I was created to do something great in life, even as a little girl. As a child, I saw more in other people than I could see in myself. I remember in school just encouraging people. I recall a classmate who got bullied every day. They would talk about her clothes and call her hurtful names. One day, I walked over to her and encouraged her because I saw tears falling down on her face. I cheered her up and talked to her about God.

The older I got, the more I noticed that my household was different from other households. There wasn't a male figure in our home. The first time I saw my father was really brief. I believe I was five or six years old. I would sometimes talk to my dad on the phone, but we really did not have a close bond. My father and my mother were distant with each other because of unresolved issues from things that occurred before I was born. Sometimes my father would call my mother's house, and she would allow me to speak to him on the phone. I remember the feeling of excitement that would come over me. I did not spend time with my father often, but when we talked on the phone I valued every moment.

One day—I believe I was about nine years old—my dad called with an urgent message about his mother being sick, and he wanted me to see her. I didn't recall ever meeting my grandma on my dad's side before. I remember talking to my dad on the phone, but I didn't quite understand what was going on. He wanted to pick me up and take me to see my grandma, but my mom told him it was too late for me to go out. Shortly after, I received a call saying my grandma had passed away. I didn't know how to respond because I was too young to understand death.

After my grandma passed away, I spoke to my father less. Before, we didn't talk on a regular basis, and now we had not talked for weeks. Weeks turned into months and months into years.

My mother would sometimes go overboard with material stuff—cute clothes, hairstyles, and money—but it did not fill the void I had on the inside. My mother felt bad because she knew how much I desired to have a closer relationship with my dad. I remember watching some of my cousins' fathers being active in their lives. I desired to spend time with my father—grabbing ice cream and going to father-daughter dances. My father was there financially, but oftentimes I wanted a more personal relationship. I wanted to be validated and feel safe as a young girl. Every little kid wants and needs their father.

The feeling of emptiness brewed inside of me. I felt it heavy as a child and was silent with a lot of mixed feelings and unanswered questions. I felt like something was missing. I oftentimes felt like I wasn't good enough. However, my mother always found ways to be positive about my father and our relationship. She also kept me active in school and church activities.

Even as a single mom, my mother had a great amount of support from my grandma and some of her siblings. My grandma Mrs. Thang took me under her wings and poured into me. She taught me about God and how important it is to establish a relationship with God. This caused friction between some of the family members and myself. They became jealous and envious of me.

Around the age of 9 or 10, my mother wanted me to go to a good school, but she was not in the school district. So, she allowed me to stay with one of her family members who lived in the area of the catholic school that my mother wanted me to attend. As a child, I remember having some of the best times around my family, but later on I started to witness jealousy, envy, strife, slander, clicks, and division amongst some of our family members. I noticed that my mother was treated differently from some of her siblings. I was mistreated and remained silent about the verbal and physical abuse going on in the family. The disrespectful conversations about my mother took place in front of me. Like any child, your first defense is to defend your parents, but they dared me to say anything to my mother about what I had heard. There were a lot of curse words, harsh conversations, and false judgements. Some words were so hurtful that they affected my psychological growth and shaped me into a young girl with a complex. Some things were hard to forget, and I did not feel good about who I was and who my mother was.

This behavior from family members continued for many years, and then one day I became bold enough to let my mother know what was going on. My mother and her closest sister Cookie were my safe haven.

I felt safe and open to share how I was feeling and what was going on in my world. My aunt Cookie and I were extremely close and oftentimes I felt empowered around her. Every opportunity that she had she made me feel loved and accepted. I told them about a conversation I had heard, at another aunt's house, about how I was conceived. It was said that I was an accident baby. When I told my mother she was definitely upset and denied any of the false information. She then confronted the family members and shortly after moved me out of their house. For many years as a young girl, I thought I was a mistake and did not belong.

Shortly after, my mother started beauty college, and I started spending more time at my grandma's house. One year, I begged my mother to let me stay with my grandma and go to school from her house, and my mother allowed it. When I was at my grandma's house it was one of the best years that I have ever experienced. I was surrounded by so much love, laughter, peace, and the word of God.

At one point I started journaling. Not often, but I would write down what was going on in my life and how it affected me. As a young girl, I remember visualizing a bright future. I started writing down what I thought were just words. I was so specific in what I was writing. I wrote down where I wanted to see myself in the future. I felt so much relief after putting my feelings on paper. My environment cultivated and inspired me to write down my goals and aspirations.

As I got older, I was around my mother a lot watching everything she did. My mother would wake up every morning, bathe, put makeup on her face, and pick out some fashionable clothes. I used to think my mother was so dope and admired her creativity. She shopped at Saks Fifth Avenue and purchased trendy clothes. Her outfits were always color coordinated with her purses and accessories. Her fingernail and toe polish even matched. I told myself at 10 years of age that I was going to be a boutique owner or fashion designer. I always saw my mother take interest in herself as a woman. I wanted to grow up and be a woman who also dresses up and feels good about herself. That's when I really started to discover my passion in life, and today, I love everything about the beauty and fashion industry.

I remember reaching a point in my life where I became extremely interested in fashion. I would take clothes that my mother had bought me and redesign the whole outfit. I remember the first time I got put on punishment for that. My mother had bought me a brand-new outfit, and I put rips in the jeans and redesigned the shirt. When my mother mentioned it to my grandma she just laughed and said to her, "You took on fashion, but she is taking fashion to the next level with a twist."

Mom replied, "It looks good on her now that I think about it." My mother started to realize that this fashion journey I was on was more than a phase—it was my purpose. Later on, my grandma and I visited a church and there a prophet told me that I was going to be a fashion designer and boutique owner, and one day I would have my own clothing line that was going to bless the Christian community.

Even all through school, for as long as I can remember, I would get compliments on my outfits. I was really big on how I wanted to feel in my clothes. Sometimes people thought my mother was putting my outfits together because she was really big on keeping my hair together since she was going to hair and beauty college.

As a child, my mother was the best! Christmas in our house was major. My mother went above and beyond with Christmas tree decorations, tasty desserts, and a delicious meal. My mother was a giver so oftentimes she bought gifts for her siblings and some of their children and for family members that couldn't afford it. Christmas and Thanksgiving in our house were times of giving and enjoying family. Although my mom was a single parent, she gave me more than enough—sometimes a little too much, and I was always so excited. Some of my cousins would call me and ask what I got.

"Hey, what did you get for Christmas"?

With excitement, I replied, "I got a Baby Alive, Barbie dolls, a Barbie doll house and…."

After naming all my gifts, I remember hearing silence over the phone. There was no excitement on their part. They only seemed disappointed as they mentioned only getting one toy. I would then feel bad for even mentioning what I got for Christmas. What was innocent excitement from a child was then used by the enemy as a tool to plant seeds of envy and jealousy. My excitement was considered bragging to them, but I didn't realize it at the time.

Like my mother, I was compelled to be a giver. I would give away outfits, shoes, etc. However, even in my efforts of giving, it didn't change or deter them from being jealous of me because of my material possessions. Although my mama raised me as a single parent, she still encouraged me and stood behind me, and I had some cousins who weren't getting that at home.

During my fifth-grade year, my mother moved to a nice neighborhood. I was the new girl on the block, and I was extremely shy. We moved into a nice three-bedroom apartment and we lived there for years. Right away my mother enrolled me in a new elementary school where I met a couple of friends. I was so excited to make a friend because I barely knew anybody in that area. As the new kid on the block people tried to bully me because I was so quiet. Even though I was a lover and not really a fighter, fighting was how I was conditioned. My mother was strict, and the only time I was able to be a little free was when I went to one of my auntie's houses.

Since I was such a grandma's baby, I convinced my mother to let me go to school near my grandmother's house. At the time my grandma lived in Mt Airy, so I started attending Mt. Airy School where I met some of my closest friends Trina and Shay. Trina and I became extremely close. She was really genuine and we had so much in common. Because I was shy and quiet, I was bullied and had my first fight in elementary school. I was afraid that I was going to be grounded, but the teacher never reported the fight, and I was so grateful. I stayed at Mt Airy until my 6th grade year and transitioned to junior high school in the fall. That summer my grandmother moved to the Westwood area and I went to school in my mother's neighborhood.

I remember being mishandled and mistreated by family members and friends, which left emotional scars on my heart. Betrayal was the norm. Not trusting was the norm. It was hard to really get used to healthy behavior. I had a male cousin who had a really bad temper. He used to put his hands on me and other females, including his mom. He hit me several times until one day when I got fed up and decided to fight back. We were at a relative's house, and he just caught me on the wrong day. He hit me and I just started swinging on him. This was the first time I fought a male. He hit me so hard in my head that he kind of dazed me.

Later on, this male cousin continued doing malicious things to me. I was terrified of dogs and he knew I was. I believe I had to be about 12 years of age. I was walking through the woods looking for one of my friends when I heard someone behind me. I turned around and saw my cousin trying to sic his dog on me. All I remember is hearing the dog bark and him charging at me.

I yelled, "Please stop! I'm scared!"

He just chuckled and said repeatedly, "Get her," as the dog continued charging at me.

After repeatedly asking my cousin to stop, he finally listened but continued to laugh as tears rolled down my face. I ran out of the woods and went home to tell my mom what had happened.

The older I got the more I realized that I had gotten used to being treated badly. I couldn't decipher what was healthy and authentic love because, one moment I was around love, and the next moment I was around slander, backbiting, animosity, jealousy, competition, and envy amongst family members. Every time I went back home from family functions my mother had to reteach me to get me back on track.

I had a good, deep conversation with my mother concerning my feelings about how I was treated when I went to certain family members' houses. As a child, I thought that what I saw and felt was normal. But, as I got older I became vocal about not being okay with the things that were causing me to have insecurity issues, confidence issues, and rejection issues. The older I got the more I realized that I felt a lack of value and purpose.

CHAPTER 3

Surviving My Teenage Years

Looking for Love

AS A TEENAGER, I REMEMBER FEELING LIKE LOVE DIDN'T EXIST. My bad experiences made me doubt that I was worthy of love. When I questioned certain people's actions towards me, they would oftentimes say, "That's all I know!" So, I thought that was the way life was supposed to be. The truth is those same individuals were just giving me excuses for their poor behavior, instead of taking accountability for their actions. As a result, later I had to learn how to filter through mental and emotional damage.

Dealing with rejection and abandonment issues at a young age, I became a major introvert. I was socially withdrawn and very awkward. I did not know how to have a healthy dialogue with my peers. I lived in fear, afraid to trust and to simply be authentically me because of the patterns of betrayal I had already experienced at such an early age.

There were so many times in my life I felt out of place. I wanted to be loved and accepted by family and peers, so I altered myself. I learned how to adapt in unhealthy environments in order to go along with the crowd or try to fit in.

I realized that I wasn't being true to myself. However, the feeling of not being good enough was a seed that was planted in me as a child. Because of status, looks, and abandonment issues, I felt like something was wrong with me. I felt different and not pretty enough. My mom would oftentimes tell me that I was different because I was unique, and that God had a special purpose for me. But, I still wasn't happy. I remember asking God, "Why can't I be the girl with the long hair and the perfect shape?" I was getting picked on by family members and peers because of my weight, and I was fed up! I was tired of being teased, so I made changes, not for me, but for everyone else. I just wanted to fit in. It also bothered me a lot because I didn't have two active parents.

At 13 years old, I didn't like myself and my insecurities took control of my life. Tired of being the short, heavy-set girl, I practically starved myself. I just really got tired of how I looked and wanted to do something about it. I wanted to be the image of my peers. Plus, I had a crush on a very cute light skinned guy. I wanted him to like me, but he was not interested in me. He told me that I was too thick for him. I was so crushed and even more determined to lose weight then. So I went on a diet and lost a total of 25 pounds within 2 weeks. My mom, who was so worried at this point, asked me, "What's wrong? Is everything okay?"

I said, "Yes Mom." My mother was still very concerned about me, but I was more excited about the amount of weight I had lost. I explained to my mom about a diet I had heard about from my friends. I said, "I was tired of being the chubby kid and I wanted to change my image, Mom."

I went back to school and the same guy I had a crush on asked me out. As a young girl, I was so excited about the attention I was receiving. My new look caused a positive boost in my self-esteem, but I dealt with backlash from family members and friends. For instance, one day while walking down the street with some of my female cousins, guys started noticing me. My cousins became jealous because they were used to getting all the attention. I even recall one time getting into a disagreement with a cousin. She told me that I thought I was better than her, but it was definitely false. I was just so glad to make this transformation in my life. It was not easy always being overlooked by people and feeling as though I didn't meet the standards of my peers.

Being violated

Since I didn't have any friends in our new neighborhood or any siblings my age, some weekends my mother would allow me to spend the night with some of my relatives so I could play with my cousins. One weekend during the summer, I spent the night over a relative's house, and met up with my best friend Trina and a cousin that lived close by in the neighborhood. My best friend and I went to elementary school together, so seeing her was exciting. We had so much in common and I finally had a friend I could be myself around. This particular summer we became so close that we started calling each other cousins.

Every time I was at this particular family member's house, my friend Trina and I would hang out. We would play outside, make up songs, do each other's hair, and dress up. One particular weekend we met up again and decided to walk around the neighborhood because it was nice and warm outside. We were outside for hours dancing and singing, just doing what 14-year-old teens do. We walked to the store where I met my first boy crush. I was so excited. He was very cute, light-skinned with hazel eyes.

I remembered that I was told to be in the house before it got dark. So after leaving the store, I got back to my family member's house around 7:30 pm, and my cousin and Trina went home. As I walked in the house safely, I locked the door behind me. My crush called me as soon as I got in the house and we talked for hours. I felt like I was falling in love with him. He was generous, respectful, and cute. I just enjoyed our conversation. I thought I was in love even though I lacked the knowledge of what love was.

Shortly after getting off the phone, there was a knock at the door. I asked who it was. It was one of my cousins, so l let him in. I really didn't think anything of it because he was family.

As I sat on the couch, he sat on the other end. He started having inappropriate conversations with me like telling me how good sex feels. I thought to myself that it was kind of strange for him to be having a conversation concerning this topic with his own female cousin. But, I wasn't really taking him seriously because I was still thinking about the guy I had just talked to on the phone.

Even though I felt that the conversation was odd, I never in a million years thought that night would change my whole life. The conversations became more intense, and I was definitely caught off guard. The more he talked about it, the more uncomfortable I felt in his presence. He then asked me, "Do you want to know how sex feels"? I looked puzzled because I was only a teenage girl who had no knowledge about sex. I was only experiencing puppy love.

Then he moved close to me. Since he was tall, he picked me up in the air. I asked him, "What are you doing?"

He said, "I am about to show you how sex feels."

"No! Put me down!" I responded.

At this point I knew he was serious. He put me on the bed and started pulling down my bottoms as I was trying to pull them back up. I repeatedly asked him to stop, but he continued to put his body weight on me. I remember not being able to fight anymore as he continued to violate me. I felt voiceless. It was like I couldn't speak.

Afterward, I was numb and confused. I couldn't wrap my mind around what had just happened. He then told me, "Don't tell anybody."

I didn't know at the time how keeping that secret was going to damage me. I remember having so many mixed emotions and feeling disgusted. I ran to the bathroom, looked at myself in the mirror, and hated myself. I felt sick to my stomach and wanted to vomit, but nothing came up. I began wiping my private area. I realized I was bleeding a little and got scared. I began to panic and all kinds of thoughts ran through my head. I asked myself, "Am I pregnant? Will my mom suspect anything?" Every day after that I was so afraid that I might be pregnant.

Since my relative, who owned the house, was at work at the time, there was no one to protect me. That night turned out to be one of the most painful experiences of my life. I felt betrayed, hurt, and useless. I didn't tell anyone about what had happened and hid it for years.

My virginity was taken away from me that night, and I had no say so, nor the power to stop it. I remembered my grandma's and mother's teachings about taking care of my temple. My body was a temple, and I was supposed to wait for the right time to give myself to my future husband, but I was robbed of my innocence that night.

I was afraid of my cousin after that night. Besides, he was tall and heavy set, and I was kind of petite. Plus, I was only in my teens, and he was at least three years older than I was.

I went on with life like normal, while keeping this painful secret to myself. I started blaming myself for what happened to me. I felt like I could have fought a little harder, but because of fear I was afraid to defend myself more. I also blamed myself for completely changing my appearance and dropping weight. I said to myself, "Maybe I was asking for it!" I questioned if God loved me or not. I didn't understand why bad things continued to happen to me.

My cousin was known for having a violent background. Also, I knew if I opened up about being violated, I could potentially ruin my mother's relationship with her sister Ann. It became harder to cope with what happened to me.

I hated myself

After the sexual abuse, my self-esteem was completely destroyed. I went into a deep depression and struggled with suicidal thoughts. I isolated myself from everyone in the house and spent a lot of time alone in my room. I silently cried out for help. I said, "Lord why me? Why do I have to experience a life of trauma after trauma?" I even compared my situations to people that I felt had a healthier lifestyle or just a normal family. My family, at times, seemed loving, but the continual betrayal and hatred caused me to despise the word "family". As a child, I visualized this amazing lifestyle, but my reality was far from it. I just wanted to be loved and to have a safe place to be valued and protected.

Acting out

I remember becoming tough. I was crying out for help, but no one knew it. While silently suffering, I camouflaged myself in public by smiling and acting like everything was alright. I started hanging out more with some of my female cousins. We constantly fought in school and in different neighborhoods. If my cousins were fighting, then I was fighting. I didn't care!

After summer break was over, I started junior high. The first week of school, some girls followed me halfway home from school and jumped me. I did not get too many bruises, and just a few scratches. As soon as I got home, I told my mother what had happened and she was upset, but at that point I had already made up my mind that I was going to stand up for myself and not allow anyone to put fear in me. I was numb to pain. I was bitter and angry inside and it was starting to show.

Blocking out the hurt

The following summer when I was around 15 years old, I sneaked out to the club with one of my aunts. Since I was underage, I got spotted by a policeman and was sent to 20/20 which is a juvenile detention center in Cincinnati, Ohio. My mother was notified and had to pick me up. I remember the disappointed look on her face, but that wasn't enough to slow me down.

I went on with life as normal, not realizing that my life wasn't normal. Even though the painful traumatic experiences didn't go away, I just found ways to mask it. I started hanging out with a group of girls that wasn't for me. I did not have good judgment of character. I felt like everyone was my friend at the time, even though I sensed that some people had the wrong intentions for being my friend. They had many hidden agendas, but I was willing to tolerate the bad company just to feel accepted. A lot of friends were trying to connect with me because I had something valuable to bring to the friendship.

Pain was pushing me towards my passion

Because I was acting out, my mother had to ground me more. However, spending more time at home allowed my creative side to come out. Even though I was suffering silently, I started to tap into the many gifts God had placed inside of me.

When I moved to the Fay Apartments I discovered my niche, passion, and possibly my purpose. Around the age of 15 is when I started putting more actions into the things that I enjoyed doing. Beauty and fashion were a very essential part of my culture. I was inspired by so many people in my life, especially my mother, some of my aunts and my mentor. They were really fashionable and I admired different fashion sense styles. I even started putting more energy into my hair. Neighbors noticed my hairstyles and asked, "Who did your hair?" They were shocked to hear that it was me. So, people started knocking on my door asking me to do their hair, and I said yes. Word about my skills spread throughout the neighborhood, and I was able to build up my clientele without a hair license. I had so many clients that I even had to turn some away. I loved doing hair. I enjoyed encouraging women with low self-esteem and making them feel beautiful. My best friend and I did hair in my mother's kitchen and got clients every week for the entire summer.

I started singing when I was a young girl. The older I got the more singing became the way I release what was bottled up inside of me. Singing was like therapy to me and it is the way I responded to my pain. When I sang it was like I had no pain or problems because I would empty every emotion in whatever song I would sing. Whether I was at home, on the streets, or in a church setting, singing allowed me to be free.

I oftentimes sang solos at my church whenever my grandma was preaching. Two of her favorite song selections were "Because of Who You Are" and "I Love You". When I was in church, I would close my eyes and worship God, giving him my all. I started writing songs and realized I wanted to be a singer. I wrote several songs with family and friends with the goal of one day creating a gospel record. Music was really big on my mother's side of the family as well as on my dad's side of the family. My father was in a band and he managed a band. That's when I realized that my father and I had music in common.

One day while walking home from school, I was singing, and this young man stopped me and asked me to be a part of a major record label in Cincinnati. He had a sister that was already in an established rap group called OTR. I took his business card and told him I would get in touch with him soon. I was excited! I told my mother about what just happened, and she told me to follow my dreams and that she supported me on every positive idea I wanted to do.

Being broken while trying to tap into your purpose is not easy. For instance, I got the opportunity to sing on Media Bridges which was a televised platform that brought exposure to upcoming artists. My cousins and I performed in front of the world on Media Bridges. I sang the chorus and they rapped. I also sang the first song I wrote called "I Need You Lord". It was a powerful song that helped me through difficulties in life. But eventually what was on the inside began to show more and more on the outside. I could hide my pain no longer. I knew that I was not in the right mental space, so I had to put music on hold.

Feeling insecure and never good enough, I started to shelter myself from people. At this point, I did not have enough faith in myself and the credibility of people. I stopped pursuing my music because I felt like my vocals weren't good enough.

The betrayal

I remember my grandma trying to bring the family together in unity but never seeing it happen because envy and jealousy made it impossible to do. Even though I didn't see unity in our family, I still had a strong desire to see us love on each other. I thought to myself," We are family, and we should be able to come together."

Oftentimes, my mother would tell me, "Baby I know you want to be loved and accepted, but some of your cousins are jealous of you." But I didn't listen and found out the hard way. Seeing competition and comparisons in my family was disheartening. A few of my cousins came to me personally and told me that they did not like me. When I asked why, their response was, "You are treated better, and your mother buys you everything." So, as a young girl and as a teenager, I would sometimes take my last dollar to bless them, but it was never good enough. I continued this unhealthy cycle for many years. I would allow others to inflict their insecurities on me. I was walking in the spirit of rejection and letting people who were supposed to love me mistreat me. Rejection and abandonment were perpetual and continued to resurface in my life. Every time I thought I was healed from the spirit of rejection it would show up in another area, form, or situation in my life.

Oftentimes, I felt like we were the black sheep of the family. I dealt with a lot of situations that were unfavorable to me growing up. I had little to no confidence in people which caused trust issues and made it hard for me to connect with others. I stayed away from building connections with females because of my years of dealing with toxic behaviors and betrayal from family and friends. I remember some of my female cousins would intentionally talk to the same guys I was talking to, or negatively slander my name because of jealousy. So, oftentimes I would gravitate to my male cousins. We would have a ball going to the show and going on double dates. You name it, we had a ball! Some of my male cousins and I were extremely close.

I now realize that the root of the love-hate relationship amongst my cousins was because the toxic and competitive relationships among our parents were deeply rooted. As children we watched those behaviors as we sat up under our parents while they gossiped about other family members and disrespected one another.

I remember God using my mother as a prophet to tell me things that she saw about the people I was connected to, hoping that I would be smart enough to make corrections accordingly. But I just wanted to be accepted. I had extremely poor judgment concerning people because I always saw the best in others. Sometimes I would self-sabotage my own life. I got so used to the rejection, that I started embracing it.

Around the age of 16, I started to show interest in guys. Even though I had toxic relationships with some of my cousins, I still hung around them. Because of their jealousy they tried to sabotage me. For instance, I hooked one of my cousins up with my boyfriend's cousin only to find out that my cousin and her sister talked badly about me behind my back.

As a cousin, I was so hurt. My mother had seen right through their behavior and tried to shelter me from the jealousy, but, as a teenager, it seemed like I was always the target. When I found out that a few of my cousins were talking to the same guys I was talking to, I couldn't understand it. As family, we were not supposed to date each other's boyfriends, but I seemed to be the only one that respected the code. People thought I was this perfect princess, but deep inside I was empty. Although I was in pain, I dressed my pain up well.

I remember when I told my mother that a few of our relatives really despised her and mistreated me because of how they felt about my mother. One particular relative named Ann had said and done some of the most hurtful things to me that no adult should ever do or say to a child. She told me when I was 12 years old that I was conceived by inappropriate sexual behavior. My mother said that those rumors stemmed from jealousy and animosity, and it wasn't correct. In fact, she let me know that my dad and she both loved me very much, but agreed to go their separate ways and co-parent.

Some memories are more painful to forget. For example, I remember going to Ann's house for the weekend. I was told to wash the dishes shortly after my mother left. When I put my hands in the water, I took them out quickly, because the water was scalding hot." I said, "Hey Aunt Ann, this water is too hot!" She cursed at me and told me to wash the dishes. She knew that the water was too hot, but forced me to wash the dishes anyway., I couldn't understand the reason for my aunt's harsh behavior towards me. As a child, I remember my aunt allowing her children to lay around the whole time while I did their chores. I felt like this was completely wrong. I realized that my silence was paralyzing me and keeping me stuck in a place of pain and defeat. So, I started naming all of the offensive behaviors that were done to me, including slander, lies, abuse, and manipulation.

For as long as I could remember, Ann continued trying to destroy my mother's and her children's names. The continuous jealousy caused rivalries and vendettas amongst family members. I began telling my mother how her unhealthy relationships with some of the family members had contributed to the brokenness going on inside me. Now was the time for me to use my voice to speak up about all the abuse and slander that had crippled me from progressing forward in life. I also told my mother how Ann had justified every foolish behavior that her children had done to me and that she was continuing to spread lies and speak negatively against me. I told my mother that Ann did not have good intentions. I had outgrown the foolishness and was not going to allow it to continue in my life.

Growing up around family

Growing up, the family got together for everything, from big family barbeques to going to Sunday church services. We had a big family and oftentimes we had a lot of family gatherings and outings. My grandma was the rock of the family and her goal was that we, as a family, establish a relationship with God and love one another.

At one point of my life, I felt like my family was the best, but in reality, there were family secrets and disrespect amongst relatives. I remember still having to show up around the cousin who had violated me and no one in the family knew about it, not even my mom. I had learned that some things had to be overlooked in order to keep the family together. Like myself, oftentimes the children were caught in between unresolved controversy. However, the good days were when my grandma held everything together. She preached about love, unity and how making things right with one another was the godly thing to do. As a pastor, my grandma continued to pray for the family. Her main prayer was that we would all give our lives to Christ before it was too late.

Growing up in a house with a mother who has a prophetic gift was not easy. God showed her so much. I watched my mother deal with many oppositions in her life because of the calling on her life. She was the one who would bless and help anyone in need, especially family. My mother was a caregiver by heart. She would take care of people who were no longer able to take care of themselves. So, the persecution and slander that she endured at the hands of family members angered me. It was a continuous cycle. Sometimes, when I thought my relatives had changed, the same behavior continued to happen.

As I got older, I did not want to be around jealous and envious people, especially the ones who were using my mother. I can recall her helping and assisting people with rent money and other bills. Several times she allowed people to live with her until they got on their feet. As a young lady, I spoke up and asked my mother, "Mom why do you continue to allow some of your relatives to leech off of you and not respect you?"

My mother responded, "God always blesses me." This answer would always frustrate me because what I saw affected how I looked at my family. My mother did not understand that the message I was receiving at the time was that it was acceptable to allow people to mistreat you. I was learning how to accept unhealthy behaviors in my life. Sometimes God would show me who wasn't for me or who was against me, but I would turn a blind eye.

By the time I was a young woman, God really started opening my eyes and allowing me to use my voice to break generational cycles. It was so important not to normalize trauma in the family and manipulate children with God's word. I had watched the scripture "honor your mother and father" used so habitually only to continue to provoke children to anger, low self-esteem, abuse, and slanderous talk. This was damaging to myself and some of my cousins. We became products of our environment. Growing up I was forced to forgive behaviors and offenses without the proper healing. Forgiveness is necessary, but relatives who cause emotional distress must also be held accountable. Setting boundaries and making people respect them are important. It's not okay to get violated by a family member and then have to fellowship with that same relative at family barbeques. As a young girl, I couldn't set boundaries on my own, but as a young adult, I had to set the record straight. No matter who they were, if they had caused me mental and physical harm I was not going to be in their presence.

Gossiping and backbiting were the norm in the family. Some relatives made it hard for unity and togetherness to happen. Relatives started distancing themselves from family members because of animosity and family beef. Some stayed away completely because the drama was too much. It was like a continuous cycle.

Oftentimes I internalized things because I did not know who to trust. I held onto the pain from the mental, verbal, and physical abuse I endured growing up. The older I got, the more I embraced pain and became angry.

Growing up, I saw how my younger cousins were physically and mentally abused by their parents and how the abuse affected their development. Those scars showed up in their everyday lives. They were silently suffering in dysfunction. Like myself, they couldn't get away, and there was no safety net to protect them from all the trauma they were experiencing.

During my youth, I struggled with the fact that I did not have a close relationship with my dad. Although I felt hurt, I came to the conclusion that having my mother in my life was enough. I convinced myself to move on and continue living life. I wanted to forget about the things that were hurting me.

I really got tired of going to family members' houses where they felt the need to mistreat my siblings and me because of the animosity they had against our mother. I watched my mother bless relatives who did not say thank you. I was growing to resent my family more and more. At this point I realized that family is not just blood, but it is people who treat you like family. Many times I heard disrespectful conversations about my mother, and I would ask her why she continued to allow these dysfunctional cycles in her life. Her response was always, "Momma told us to stay together." Knowing healthy relationships was extremely hard for me because I had not seen any in my life.

I had a couple of relatives who were more verbally abusive with their words than others. When certain relatives first started calling me harsh and disrespectful words, I would get so offended because I was not used to hearing those words in my home. My mother was strict, but slanderous talk wasn't a way she disciplined me. Although I would get mad, I was raised in the era where children weren't allowed to talk back to adults, so I could not say how I was feeling. Being disrespectful wasn't allowed from any of the children, even if the parents were wrong. We weren't allowed to have freedom of speech, even if something was hurting and offending us. I was raised to allow my mother to handle it. Oftentimes I did mention it, but other times I did not in order to keep the peace between Mom and her siblings.

My mother had this amazing sister named Cookie. I loved my aunt Cookie so much. When I lived on Elm Street and my aunt Cookie lived in Mt Auburn I would get dropped off at her house. Whenever I went to my auntie's house, I would have a ball. Her house was a safe haven where I could wind down and release my thoughts to her. My auntie edified and encouraged me all the time. She showed me so much love that any feelings I had of feeling unloved diminished. She made going to the store feel like a field trip. If I went to her house after school, she would give me $15.00, and I would then walk to my aunt Jamie's house. As a child, receiving $15.00 was a lot, so I used to think my aunt Cookie was wealthy. I really admired and looked up to her. She was a hard-working mother and a dedicated woman who pursued her dreams. I remember expressing to my aunt what it was like going to some of my other family members' houses. For example, I had one male cousin who despised me while I was growing up. He would oftentimes beat on me and my mother had to correct his behavior over and over. One day while walking home from school, he put his hands on me. One of my mother's friends saw it and called my mother to tell her. My mother confronted this cousin. She told him, "You are not going to keep putting your hands on my daughter. You are not her father." It then became a dispute with his mother. So, the dysfunctional family issues continued and led me down the road of depression.

Sexual Harassment

Sexual harassment is never okay, but as a teen girl in junior high it happens every day. What was really important to me as a teen was to fit in and be accepted. When I started going to junior high school during the fall season, I was kind of nervous because I was going into a new environment and the school was extremely big. Once I switched my classes, everything changed. I was in classes with classmates who were a little older and more mature, experience-wise. Some of the guys were older because they were repeating the same grade. Later, I was switched to an accelerated class with the goal of getting promoted to some high school programs early. The Cambridge program was a program for junior high/high school transitional classes, and some of my homework went toward high school classes.

The following week, I met two young ladies who complimented my outfit. We kicked it off well and we began hanging outside of school. They became my dressing buddies and close friends. Being the new girl in a new neighborhood and school is not easy. I felt I had a lot to prove. It was either you get jumped into a gang or hang out with a crew that was semi-popular. My friends were extremely beautiful popular girls, so we attracted a lot of attention—good and bad. We would share heels, dress up and hang out. Every Friday we would go to Northgate Mall to shop and oftentimes, people would mistake us for being grown because of the way we dressed. I remember one day after school when my friends and I went shopping. We each bought a sunflower dress that was knee length. The next day we wore our dresses. We simply loved fashion!

I was so into fashion that every day I would freestyle an outfit and people would compliment me on my outfits and hairstyles. I would go to school with one outfit on and change at my friend's house because I wanted to dress like a high school student. Since I wanted attention, I was getting it but not the right attention.

Dating in junior high was very popular. All my friends were dating. I even met a guy who became my boyfriend and life was great! Of course I was not willing to lay down with him so that relationship lasted only two weeks. I was getting the attention because oftentimes I would dress older. I also became more popular because of my hairstyles and clothes.

While walking with my friends one day, I came across this guy that was really interested in me, but I wasn't feeling him at all. He would show up and walk behind me every day when I came to school. He was so used to getting what he wanted. Some days I felt like he was stalking me. The first time he touched me inappropriately was during the changing of bells. I saw him trying to approach me, so I tried to go in the opposite direction, but the halls were crowded. He had a bond roller and stuck it up my dress.

I checked him real good, but he didn't stop his offensive behavior. Daily he kept trying to get me to go out with him, but I avoided him every time. I was so tired of getting harassed. I really felt that he was disrespectful and I did not like him.

One day he stopped me and said, "Hey baby what's up with you"? as he laughed in front of his boys.

I replied, "I'm not interested in you."

He got extremely upset because I rejected him. So, he replied, "Forget you!" He then cursed at me and spit on me.

At this point I was beyond angry and got pulled into the office. I called my mom and yelled, "Mom he spit on me! I can't believe that he disrespected me like this!"

Junior high was starting to become a hostile environment for me. This guy was not happy with being rejected, so he became more disrespectful and it caused even more problems. I went home and told my mom exactly what happened, and she started shouting and using vulgar language. At this point she was tired and was on her way to the school. I begged my mom not to go. I said, "I will reach out to the principal about the matter." As a teenager it was not easy telling authorities about harassment, bullying, and just typical teenage drama because it showed a sign of weakness. I felt like I was mature enough to deal with the issues that occurred surrounding my peers. But I was wrong. At the time I tried to rationalize why he would not back off and stop harassing me. Word at the school was that he always treated other young girls that way and somehow he felt like it was appropriate to treat me the same way. I was not having it. I was destined to be different.

The next morning at school I was kicking it with my friends and talking about our weekend plans. I left class about ten minutes early hoping he would not notice I was gone, but surprisingly he was with his homeboy. He was aggressive and had an attitude. He seemed to think that he should get everything he wanted. I called my mom and she responded, "What?! I am on my way! I am tired of this nonsense! I hope he doesn't think that you don't have family!"

Within the next ten minutes my male cousins pulled up to the school ready to fight. The policeman escorted my family and me off the premises. I went home with so many mixed emotions. I felt confused, violated, oppressed, and angry. I could not understand why this harassment situation was getting out of control.

After Mom talked to the board of education, she decided to put me in homeschool. Homeschool seemed like the best decision for me at the time. However, while my mom was at work, I was at home with major idle thoughts going on in my mind. I was different. I was not myself. I was an emotional wreck spending a lot of time in my bedroom. At this point, I felt so much in my heart. Matter of fact, hate was an understatement. I felt like I was always dealing with pain and trauma and I could not catch a break. I felt like if I had run into the boy who had harassed me, I would have done physical harm to him. With so many mixed emotions going on in my mind I became really depressed. Since I was homeschooling, a lot of my friends were asking about me, but they had no clue what was going on at the time and I was too ashamed to tell them. So due to my growing depression from the rape and sexual abuse, I finished the rest of my junior high school year at home. I was in my room for half of the day crying. I even had suicidal thoughts not wanting to be here anymore.

CHAPTER 4

My Battles With Depression

DEPRESSION IS REAL. AT THE TIME I DID NOT REALIZE WHAT I WAS struggling with, but I knew something was completely off with my mental health. I was extremely emotional, withdrawn, and angry all the time. After seeing a therapist, I was diagnosed with major depression (MDD), a severe form of depression which is a combination of biological, psychological, and social distress. Oftentimes this form of depression can be caused by trauma and environmental influences. Depression was also hereditary in my family due to trauma, loss, and other traumatic experiences.

Oftentimes people mock depression, or suicide. If a person tells you that they are going to kill themselves, believe them. As a teenager, I was suicidal. I thought about multiple ways I could take myself out of this world. I had thoughts of jumping off the bridge, running in the street, and cutting my wrist. You name it, I thought about it. But God would not allow it. As a suicide survival, God delivered me from this desolate place. I am so passionate about talking about it now because I was at the face of death, but God had other plans.

I was in a tunnel unable to be reached. No number of words at that time were able to reach me. I began to isolate myself and sleep a lot so I wouldn't have to face my reality. I didn't want to continue crying myself to sleep every night, and I had only one solution left—to take my own life. Every time I tried to visualize a word of hope, the feeling of trauma and hopelessness would come heavy on my mind. The feelings of pain, rejection, and violation were playing in my head like a movie. I hated my life and myself, as the devil tormented my mind daily.

I remember one day really hearing in my mind, "You are worthless! No one loves you! You might as well take your own life!" I cried continually being reminded that suicide is an unforgivable sin, but the enemy had my mind so bad that day that I felt like I had to follow through with the plan. My heart was heavy and I had a lot of unanswered questions for God and my family like "Why is my life so hard? Why am I not good enough? Why are my father and I so distant? God, what did I do?"

That day I walked into my mother's room with my mind made up. I took a handful of a high dose of Tylenol. I had no idea how many I had actually taken. I was on a mission to take my own life. Taking the medications was the last thing I remembered.

Usually, my mother stayed out until 6:00 pm. But on this day she said that God led her to come home. She felt like something was not right with me. My mom came into the house at 4:00 pm and called my name several times, but I didn't respond. "Love!" she shouted. She then ran into my room and noticed I was passed out.

She immediately called the ambulance. They put something by my nose so that I could become conscious. The ambulance rushed me to the University of Cincinnati Hospital and into the emergency room. All I noticed was that everything was a blur, my speech was off, and the paramedics told me to keep communicating with them so I wouldn't die. There were so many doctors around and they politely told my mom to leave the hospital room and go into the waiting room as I was beginning to panic and cry.

My grandma rushed up to the hospital to comfort us and waited in the waiting area with my mother. The doctor came to the waiting area and said, "The parents of Love please report back to the room." They told my mom that I attempted to commit suicide. I had so many pain medicines in my system that they had to pump my stomach. The doctor told my mom that I almost did not make it. My mom began crying, and the doctor told her, "She cannot be released. She needs to be on suicidal watch." My mother burst into tears even more. The devil had plans to take me out, but God kept me.

I was transferred onto a suicidal watch floor. I was patted down and placed in a room with a young girl who tried to jump out of a two-story house. She had witnessed her best friend get killed right in front of her face. The next day I was assigned to a psychiatrist who met with me one on one. She was trying to figure out what led to me trying to commit suicide, but I did not respond. She then told me, "The only way you can get better is to be honest about what led you down this dark road." I was still silent. I did not want to talk to a shrink about my problems because I didn't think they cared. She continued, "What is hurting you so bad inside that made you feel like you wanted to end your life?" I started crying and telling her that I did not want to be here anymore. She replied, "What makes you say that?"

At this point is when I realized how important mental health is, and I began releasing everything that was burdening me. I said, "My other parent doesn't want me and the people I love only want to hurt me. I'm tired. My cousin violated me at the age of 14 and I've kept this secret for 2 years. I was sexually harassed in junior high school. I was spit on by a boy because I would not talk to him. My mom doesn't understand me and I don't have anybody that I can trust."

The psychiatrist looked puzzled and asked, "Hold on, when were you violated?"

I responded, "Last summer before school started."

She asked, "Did you tell your parents?"

I replied, "No, no one knows. I never mentioned it to anyone because it was painful to think about it."

She asked, "Do you mind talking about it?"

As tears rolled down my eyes soaking my shirt, I said, "I was over a family member's house while she was at work. My cousin knocked on the door and I sat on the coach and he started talking about how in love he was and how sex feels good. I thought in my head what an awkward conversation to be having with your little cousin. At 6 feet weighing 230 pounds or better, he picked me up and put me on a family member's bed and began to pull on my underwear. I was holding on to them asking him, 'What are you doing?' As I struggled to push him off, he continually placed himself inside me. I remember being numb, like 'This is not right!' I remember running to the bathroom and seeing blood in my private area. Feeling disgusted I washed up and my cousin left and my relative came back. I was nervous but was really quiet."

The psychiatrist asked me, "Do you want me to give you the chance to tell your mother or will you be ready to tell her at the family group session?"

Later, my mother and grandma came to the hospital to see me and we had a scheduled group session. I was quiet at first, but then I thought, "It's time to get this off my chest." I began to open up about the abandonment issues I had with my family and friends, the harassment at my school and being violated by my cousin. "Why did you not come to me about this? I am your mother. My job is to protect you." As I looked into her eyes, I noticed that she was very hurt about the situation. I cried continually and could not stop. The therapist gave my mom and me a box of tissues. I remember my mother's tears and the pain and anger she had on her face because she felt like she had let me down as a mother.

I did not tell my mother any of that before because I did not have enough courage to tell her what had been going on. At the age of 14, my mother and I weren't close. I always felt like we were not close enough to express what I was dealing with.

My biggest challenge was when my mother confronted my auntie Ann about what her son had done to me, which caused me even more pain. When she found out she didn't even ask me if I was okay or anything. She upheld her son, and went around the family making accusations that weren't true. The violation was so major that my family told my dad and my dad called me badgering me over the phone with questions. I was an emotional wreck. I was so uncomfortable talking to him. We were like strangers, although we had the same blood running in our veins. We crossed each other's paths, but we never connected.

Growing up, I swept everything up under the carpet because I never liked confrontation. I always wanted peace even though my peace had been invaded by what happened to me that night. My mother wanted to take it to court, and I was against it because I did not want to deal with the backlash of drama that came behind it. As a teenage girl I realized the dynamics of my family. We had always appeared to be a close Christian family and I did not want to tell my truth about being violated because it would shine a light and bring shame to my family.

I continued the counseling and moved on. Even during the healing process, I had another suicide attempt. I jumped into traffic trying to harm myself, and my cousin pulled me out of the street. Even while going through counseling the suicidal images in my head needed to be healed. I remember hearing the voice of the Lord saying, "I will not spare your life again. Your life is not yours to take.' I cried continually because I felt like I wasn't strong enough, even though I knew better as a Christian. I realized that just because I'm saved doesn't mean I am exempt from having problems.

I sometimes got caught up in the wrong relationships because I did not know my worth. For instance, I fell in love with a guy that was in a gang, knowing I was not supposed to be with him. Even though I was taught the right way, what I saw was sometimes different.

I desired love so badly and the need to be accepted. I would go the extra mile just to get ready for a party. I would then link up with my cousins and we would be out until 3:00 am sometimes.

One night, I went out with my cousins and was put in an uncompromising situation. Even as a teenager I knew I had a special gift. Oftentimes I would call it déjà vu, or intuition, but in reality, the Lord was speaking to me. I went to a party with my cousin and I really didn't feel led to go. I saw a plot that the guys were planning on violating us. The moment I understood the reason why we shouldn't go, with fear inside of me, I told the guys at the party that I had a family emergency and I needed to go right away. Not knowing if I was going to make it out alive, I grabbed my cousin because she was intoxicated and ran out of their house. This angered the guys, but the enemy's plans were canceled. As much as I rebelled against God, there were angels still protecting me.

CHAPTER 5

Pregnant At 16

I WAS GROWING UP TOO FAST AND JUST LOOKING FOR LOVE IN ALL THE wrong places. As a teenager I remember looking out the window, and talking to a guy that was four years older than me. At that time, we weren't concerned about our age difference. Matter of fact, dating older guys was the trend at the time.

Even though I wasn't really allowed to date, this older guy and I hit it off really well and we talked daily. We talked about our childhood and I felt like we understood each other. I was in love and excited to have someone that loved me, understood me, and was emotionally available when I needed him. We talked for a while over the phone, just good conversations. We used to talk for hours over the phone about serious topics like living arrangements, marriage and more. As soon as I turned 16, we became serious.

One evening I thought I was ready for intercourse. The first time we made out I got pregnant. I did not have any clue at the time until three months into the pregnancy.

I always wanted to be a mom, but I wasn't ready to be a mom so early. In the 90s every young teenager wanted a baby. It seemed like a trend then. For some it was cool. For me, it was a way for me to experience true love. I wanted my own child that could love me back. I felt like having a child would give me purpose for living.

I remember going to the doctor with my auntie Jamie on the day I found out about my pregnancy. The doctor told my aunt to step out of the room, because they wanted to keep my medical information private.

The doctor then told me that I was three months pregnant. I was so disappointed in myself. I thought, "How am I going to raise a child when I am still a child?" I had no clue how to be a mom.

The doctor said that I needed to let my parents know that I was pregnant. I began to cry and my doctor encouraged me and said that everything would be okay. She prescribed me some prenatal vitamins and reminded me to make sure I let my parents know what was going on.

When my aunt and I left the hospital I knew that I would have to let her know what the doctor had said. Back at my aunt's house I explained to her word for word what the doctor had said. I said, "I am pregnant auntie" with tears continually falling down my face.

She responded, "What did you say? How and when? Do you know who the father is"?

"Of course, I do," I responded. I then begged my auntie not to tell my mom. I was scared.

I stayed at Aunt Jamie's house for a total of three days. There were all kinds of negative thoughts going through my head. I thought to myself, "How can I raise a child? My whole life is over! Why would he believe me when I haven't spoken to him since I broke our relationship off?"

Since my ex-boyfriend and I weren't on good terms, I went through the pregnancy alone, as well as most of the beginning stages of my son's life. Once again, I felt abandoned without that male role model for my baby. The feeling of abandonment consumed me because my ex wasn't thrilled about the news of having a baby. So, I started out on this parenting journey alone.

Just before my aunt took me home I started panicking like crazy. When we got to the house she came in with me to act as a mediator because I was still afraid to tell my mom that her 16-year-old daughter was pregnant. I did not want to disappoint my mom but I felt like I was going to. My aunt started speaking and said, "Well sister, Love has something to tell you. Please listen before you react."

I looked over to my mom with fear in my eyes and said, "I am pregnant."

Mom had a shocked look and was a little hurt, but replied, "I know. The Lord showed me." She told me that my life was about to completely change, but as my mother, she would support me. She reached over and hugged me. She said, "The freedom that you have right now, you will no longer have anymore. You have to put your baby first."

The moment that I felt my baby move in my stomach was when I really realized how real my situation was. My body started to change. I recall being sick and not being able to eat certain foods. I began to have long talks about parenthood with my grandma and mother. I was afraid of the whole process, but I was thankful that I had my mother and grandma there to support me.

While dating my boyfriend, I broke up with him early on, before I found out that I was pregnant, because God had revealed some things to me about him. At an early age, I was introduced to God and knew how important marriage was in my culture. So, one night I prayed and asked God to let me not be deceived by my boyfriend. When I went to sleep I saw in a dream that my boyfriend was not being faithful. I cried and felt so disappointed. I then broke off the relationship and moved forward with my life. After receiving my answer so clearly in a dream I knew God was real. Ever since the day I asked God to not allow me to be deceived, God has kept his promise. God has even heightened my discernment.

It was so hard being pregnant because we were raised in a strict religious era at the time. News of me being pregnant, not only traveled through the family, but throughout the church. My mother's family loved seeing the worst in her, but she reversed the whole situation. She told me that she would support me until I finished school.

I remember having to break the news to my grandma. I was afraid to tell her because my grandma was a major role model in my life. My grandma wrapped her arms around me and told me it would not be easy but God would bring me through.

It seemed like when things happened in my family news traveled fast. People began to mock and judge me. It was like they were praying for my demise. One night, I lay in the bed, and cried for hours and hours. I felt as a young teenage girl that I knew better and that God would not forgive me for my sins. I cried and pleaded with God. "God, I am sorry. I know I disappointed you. Please forgive me."

The next day I felt a very intimate presence from God. I felt like the angels were lifting me up out of the dumps. I felt a sense of love and peace, and I was able to hold my head up even though all the odds were against me. It was a supernatural God experience. I literally felt the father wrap his arms around me. It was mind-blowing because I had never encountered God in this way before. I remember running and telling my grandma, who was a pastor, what I had just experienced. I knew I couldn't tell everyone because I knew they wouldn't believe me.

I knew giving up wasn't an option. God had given me hope and faith to keep going. Even though I had fallen short of the glory of God, he was the lifter up of my head, and my best days were ahead of me.

I dropped out of high school for a year because I started having pregnancy complications. I needed to take care of myself and my soon to be born baby. I was so young and didn't know what to expect from being a young parent. So, my mother put me in several positive girl groups. At that time I needed to be around other young parents so we could learn from one another. I met some great young girls that came from some painful backgrounds.

CHAPTER 6

How My Mentor Helped Change My Life

M Y MOTHER FOUGHT FOR ME IN WAYS THAT SHE DIDN'T EVEN understand by finding support systems to help equip me on my life journey. After my mother got information that I was pregnant, she signed me up for a teen pregnancy program so that my mindset could be shifted to a positive view. This group's mission was for teen mothers to become a sisterhood while influencing and connecting them to the right resources that they might benefit from. I was assigned to a mentor named Sharon. I thought Sharon was such a beautiful and strong woman. I was a little sheltered and shy when I first was assigned to my mentor, but the more I opened up the more grateful I was that God connected me to her. My mentor was extremely active in my everyday life. I remember Sharon coming to my high school and taking me to lunch, and we would talk about college, careers, etc. One day I really opened up to my mentor about who I was as a young parent and she stopped me and said, "Wow!" I was confused by that statement. She then said, "You are a well-rounded young lady, and you have a good head on your shoulders and you have a parent that really loves you. Some of the girls who are a part of this group are not as blessed to have the love and support that you have."

I started to reflect and feel grateful for what God blessed me with. Sharon said, "God is going to use your voice to inspire and influence people so do not give up." We continued to meet and started working on goal sheets and I was so grateful to accomplish those goals. One of my top priorities, after making sure my baby had everything he needed, was making sure I finished high school.

The curses spoken against my purpose and destiny by family members and people's opinions were getting the best of me, and my mentor noticed I was struggling. One day I cried to her and said, "You don't know how it feels to be pregnant at such a young age with no knowledge of how to be a parent and wondering if I will fail as a parent. I am judged every day I step outside the door. I am pregnant and my grandma is a pastor and my mom is an evangelist and I am in ministry. I feel so ashamed."

After allowing me to let all my emotions out, she asked me "Are you done?" As tears were rolling down my face, Sharon set me straight. "So, you are going to allow what people say to determine your future?!"

Suma was a group for pregnant teen mothers and teen fathers. Attending Suma group sessions and hearing other teenage girls' life experiences made me cry. Some teens were in broken homes and had been molested for years. For some teens, being pregnant meant everything to them because they now had someone that they could love and that could love them back. Other teens weren't sure if they were going to keep their babies because of mental and physical abuse. I realized that we had a lot in common. We were all feeling hurt and alone and trying to fit in by looking for love in all the wrong places.

My mentor really helped groom and shift my mindset in the right direction. It's funny how sometimes it takes someone from the outside to really reach you and influence you before transformation really happens. One day, she spoke words into my life that helped set my life on fire like, "You have the power to be what you want to be in life! Even with a child out of wedlock, you can be somebody! You are somebody's future wife, college graduate, business owner! The sky is the limit! Don't allow anyone to make you feel bad about making a decision that they don't have to live with! I want to see you in your future being the best woman you can be!"

At first, I thought to myself, "Here she goes with this preaching stuff!" But this time the information that was spoken was sinking in. She was speaking into my life words that one day would manifest. On that particular day, my life changed for the better. From that point on, I started looking at my unborn child as a blessing instead of a mistake. Even though some of the people were praying for my downfall, I wasn't worried because at that point I knew God had plans for me. The unborn child in my womb was growing and every time I felt the baby move, I got more excited because I was carrying a blessing.

One day Sharon came to me and told me "Love, you are going to do great things in life! I see it! I see you being a speaker!"

As I glanced at her quickly, I said, "I doubt that very seriously."

She responded, "Mark my words!"

Sharon always felt like I had so much to say. The Suma group was looking for speakers to encourage the teens and my mentor asked me if I would mind speaking? At first, I felt unqualified, but I've always loved encouraging people. I am naturally an encourager. I've been this way since elementary school.

I couldn't believe at the age of 16 that I was speaking in front of a room full of people, at least 25-30 people. I remember feeling so nervous, but as I began to open up my mouth God allowed the words to flow. As I glanced down at my notes a few times, I said:

"I know we all come from different walks of life. We were born into some crazy situations, but our lives don't stop here. We have opportunities ahead of us. We can go to college, or take up a trade and do things to make our children and our lives better. It's not where you came from but it's where you want to go."

I was ready to be the best because my baby had me to look up to. One day on Thanksgiving around 12:00 am after helping to prepare for the annual holiday, I remember feeling pain and it was coming from my back. The pain got so intense that I started yelling, "Mom come here! I am getting back pains back-to-back!" Mom said that was impossible because I was only 27 weeks. So, she called my grandma. When Grandma got to our house she told my mom that I was in labor and told me not to push.

The pain started moving to my butt area like I was about to have a bowel movement. As soon as we arrived at the hospital my grandma dropped me off at the front door so she could park. I was walking through the hospital by the elevators when I started pushing. Just like that, my son came out and I caught him with my spandex skirt. My mom began crying and screaming for help as the doctor rushed to lay me gently on the floor. I heard God's voice clearly say, "He will make it." Mind you, I did not know I was having a boy. This was my second encounter with God. At this point, I knew God was real. I understood that what God speaks is so, and no one could tell me anything different. At that moment I knew that God was full of compassion, mercy, and grace. I had been forgiven for my sins, but I had to learn how to forgive myself.

My son Dontae stayed in the hospital for about 6 months because he was premature. He needed to fully develop before he came home. I stayed in the hospital day in and day out to make sure I was present as a parent. Sometimes I would get told by the doctors to go home. I would sing gospel songs to my son every day, just like I did while he was in my womb.

I took a break from school for a while just until Dontae's health got better. When he was released from the hospital, he came home on oxygen. I was grateful that my son was able to come home and my focus was now on him. He needed more immediate attention. I remember thanking God for allowing my son to live and grow and pick up weight. I had met a lot of women that had babies that were in the INCU but some of those babies died before leaving the hospital. I told God, "This is your child. Lord, I give him back to you."

I took a whole year off from school. One day my mom sat down with me and said, "Daughter, now it is time to finish school and work on your goals." Before I was able to share my concerns, she said, "You have a son now. Go finish high school and then go to college and make something out of your life."

I enrolled in a fast-track high school just to complete my 12th grade year. Around that time, I got my first main job at a nursing home. I was juggling being a young parent, school and work. It was not easy because sometimes I would get home super late and still had to change diapers and give him his late-night feedings. I was pooped, but I kept reminding myself that I would be done with school soon and then I could decide what I wanted to do with my future. Although I was surrounded by support from my mother and grandma, I realized that I did not have any support at the time from my son's father, and the fact that I was a single mother began to discourage me.

As my son Dontae got older, I realized that he was a sick baby. He had asthma so bad that some days we were spending a lot of time in the hospital. Some nights the doctors would admit us, and we would have to stay overnight to make sure that he was well enough to come home. Some days I would miss school, and I was so afraid that I would get behind.

But I was blessed to have a counselor who worked with me. She gave me packages so that I could get caught up on my schoolwork in order to graduate.

I was focused on work and school, and then came the distractions. After I had my son, I rededicated my life back to the Lord and told him that I did not want any more children until I got married. So, I started talking to this young man at my job. He was very good-looking. We were crushing for a while until he asked me out. We started dating and he wanted to rush into having sex, but I wasn't ready because I did not want to compromise my relationship with God. I thought because our relationship was real that he would be willing to wait and we could grow together. He claimed he understood. However, when he got tired of me holding back on sex, he tried to humiliate me by talking to my childhood friend while trying to string me along. One of my close co-workers pulled me to the side and told me what he was doing. I was very hurt. When I went home, I cried and reflected. I cut him and my old buddy off. I then got back to focusing on my schooling.

One day I got a call from my counselor and she told me I had 24 credits and just needed to take an exit test. I was so excited! I screamed yes! I realized all that hard work had paid off. I went to school the next morning ready to take the test. I glanced at it and saw the math and began to get discouraged. But then I told myself, "I must do this for my son!" I took the test and gave it my all.

The next week I got a call that I passed my test and could come and get my cap and gown. I was so happy that none of the distractions I had faced stopped me from accomplishing my goals. I was finally finished and I was so proud of myself. I started looking at different colleges trying to find the right one. All I could think of was making something out of my life. I remember thinking and pondering about what career path I wanted to take and praying that I would be successful so that my son did not have to struggle.

I did not start school right away because I was still trying to figure out my purpose in life. So, I continued working at the nursing home while looking for a new job that was going to accommodate my schedule. I started working the first shift at White Castle and I really loved the whole family atmosphere of the company. My manager really poured into me and was always giving me positive feedback on how good of a job I was doing at the company. Within three months of working at White Castle, I was offered a shift supervisor position, with the potential of being a store manager. I politely turned the position down because it required me to work any shift and, as a single teen mother, I couldn't dedicate myself to that job offer at the time. I wanted more! As a young girl, I always wanted to grow in life, and now as a teen mother, I had to apply pressure. I just wanted more for my son than I did for myself.

One day, I said to myself, "This is not the end of my story, but the beginning of my story. So what, you got pregnant and now have a son! What are you going to do about it? It's not your past that determines your future. What are you doing now? Wipe your eyes and affirm yourself. Start speaking life into your situation."

That moment became one of the most powerful moments in my life. It was like God wiped away my tears and took the shame away. It was an encounter that I would never forget. From that day on I did not walk in shame anymore, because I knew that I was forgiven.

My journey as a teen parent had its highs and lows. Some days I felt like I had it all together and other days I felt a weight was on my shoulders. However, I knew I could do it, since I had already overcome a lot at this point. Being a single and active parent wasn't easy, but I took on this challenge by faith, as I learned to balance parenting and creating a better life for my son at the same time.

I realized my mentor was sent into my life to help me understand that there was purpose inside of me. I now understand the importance of using your voice to tell your testimony and to edify and encourage someone. I had no clue that my life was on display so that someone might witness the good, bad, and yet masterpiece of God.

CHAPTER 7

My Relationship With My Mother

M Y MOTHER WAS A GREAT PROVIDER. OFTENTIMES SHE WOULD MAKE sure she took that extra mile in everything she did for me. She made sure I was clean and presentable in public. I remember going on field trips as a little girl and my mother would pack lunch for me, not just any lunch but the best lunch. She went above and beyond for me. Growing up, I always looked up to my mom. I admired her beauty and boldness.

As a child, witnessing turmoil and trauma affected my growth and development. The older I got, I started to despise some of the environments that I was in. I felt like Mom did not understand that the unhealthy, toxic connections affected me negatively. Some of my trauma my mother did not know about, but she saw that some of the unhealthy cycles in the family, not only hurt me, but some of the other children.

My mother was very big on family. She loved and supported the family. However, as a child, I was surviving trying to mask all the mistreatment by family members that was going on in my life. Although there were some good moments, there was an inability for our family to have unity. On numerous occasions, I walked in on relatives having slanderous conservations concerning my mother and each other. It was like they wanted me to go back and tell her what was said in order to cause conflict. Oftentimes because of fear as a child I would keep my mouth closed.

I remember one friend my mother had. She was a teacher and had a whole daycare center in her home. Because dealing with children can be so time consuming and overwhelming, she began to hire help and pay them under the table. So, she hired me and a few other girls. I was so excited about getting a job and making a little money. The first day I worked for her, I learned not to like myself. In front of my mother's face, she praised me, but behind her back she damaged my spirit with her harsh words. She called me every name but my name in her house. I allowed this behavior to happen until my cousins, who were older, started working for her, too. They exposed her because they experienced this same treatment. Shortly after, I stopped working for her.

When I got to junior high school my relationship with my mom became distant because, like every teen, I felt like my parents didn't understand me. I felt this way a lot. My mom was a stickler and I felt like she only saw things her way. I grew up in an era where parents were always right even if it caused the children emotional distress. I explained how I felt, but oftentimes I was misunderstood. My mom and I started to have disagreements on how we looked at life differently. Often I would ask God, "Why do I think differently?" Sometimes I felt like a stranger in my home growing up. I was different and thought differently, even from my siblings.

When I got older, I had animosity toward my mom and I did whatever I could do to run away from my whole family. For as long as I could remember, I wanted to move out of town and get a different family. It wasn't because I wanted my family to be perfect. What I experienced concerning family gave me the wrong perception of what family is and what love looks like. What did a healthy family look like without all the resentment, jealousy, and gossip?

As a teenager, I began to create my own family. I realized that family is not about having the same bloodline, but it's about the heart and connection. So, I created genuine connections, although there were some wrong connections I had to separate myself from. Some family members would get offended because I had some friends that actually treated me like a sister. I did not always have to question their motives and integrity.

As a parent, some cycles I had to unlearn. With my children, I wanted to do things differently. I wanted to create my own healthy family inside of my home. I didn't want my children to heal from the same childhood trauma that I, not only had to unpack, but had to heal from. As a parent of three, I am not perfect, but I am willing to bring something different to my children.

I had to change my perspective concerning what my mother did or didn't do. I had to embrace the fact that she parented from what she knew. I had to remove an unrealistic burden off of her and embrace the new relationship that we built over time. I realized that mother-daughter bonding is so important and it was what I needed. Now my mom is my best friend, and we spend a lot of time together. We just really enjoy going out, shopping, praying, and supporting one another. My faith in God brought my mom and me closer together.

CHAPTER 8

My Relationship With My Father

MY RELATIONSHIP WITH MY DAD WAS REALLY DISTANT. I REMEMBER desiring to be a daddy's girl, and the fact that it never happened disappointed me. The older I got the more our relationship was inconsistent. It was extremely hard to build a relationship and spend time with him. However, I wanted to love him in a different way, not just because he was the man that brought me into the world. I wanted a father! I used to hear from others about what an amazing man he was, but I never experienced that side of him. Growing up, I would hear my step-sister brag about her relationship with my father. Finally, I stopped calling him because it bothered me, as his daughter, not having that close relationship.

I remember seeing my dad at different stages of my life. For instance, one time when I saw him around the age of 15, his friend looked at me and said I was beautiful. My dad then glanced at me and said, "Oh wow! That's my daughter! You are growing up so beautifully!"

My relationship with my father was a hit and miss. Sometimes we would connect, and other times we would lose contact with each other. I knew a little bit about my dad from phone conversations. So, as I was getting older, I desired to know his side of the family. I remember I was about 19 years of age the first time I met my dad's father. My cousin on my dad's side connected us. I was so excited! My grandfather came all the way to my mom's house to see me. I remember the first thing my grandfather said. "Wow! My granddaughter is so beautiful!" He then said, "I wish I knew you before. I would have loved you like the rest of my grandchildren and you would have wanted for nothing." I was so glad to receive so much love and at the moment I felt validated. Shortly after, my grandfather passed away.

On another occasion when I was going to college around the age of 22, my dad would make cab trips downtown where I had to catch the bus to and from college. My father would see me and speak so highly of me to his friends. He would introduce me and tell them, "This is my daughter. She's in college and she sings too. The brains and talent come from my side of the family." My dad was a businessman and a talented band player and producer. I enjoyed going downtown just to see my dad because those moments were the only connections we had.

When my dad and I talked on the phone, oftentimes he talked about the life he had created with his wife, step children and grandchildren. I used to wonder when I was going to get an invitation to barbecues and family dinners, but it never happened. It seemed like, as soon as I started talking to my dad, somehow he was gone again. For many years I played the chase game until I realized it wasn't my place to continue trying to reconnect us. But I still wanted to connect with my dad's family.

Although my father and his siblings had challenging relationships, I still wanted to get to know that side of the family, so I could get more clarity about who I was. One year, I was invited to a family reunion where I was able to meet more of the family that I didn't know. My dad wasn't present at the family reunion, but it was good to know who my family was. Even though it did not bring complete closeness, I was able to identify some of my family members if they passed by me on the street. For many years I had wanted to understand who I was, not just from my mother's side, but my father's side as well. From his family I was definitely embraced more by my uncles and met some of my aunts. I was extremely excited to be a part of this family reunion, even as an adult with children, because I never had the experience as a child growing up. I realize that every family has their issues, but I could identify with my father's side a little more. For instance, their outlook on life is different just like mine. I also learned that everyone in his family is into some form of music whether it is singing or playing a musical instrument. They are also career and goal-driven.

Dealing with painful moments in life while growing up in a single-parent home has helped me mature and not allow bitterness and unforgiveness to take root. As a Christian woman God has given me a heart of compassion to forgive and to pray even when I don't understand why I had to experience some of the disappointments I experienced. I pray for my father all the time. As an adult, the love I had for him as a little girl hasn't changed. I pray that God prospers him and, when the time is right, that we will have an amazing father and daughter relationship.

CHAPTER 9

Dealing With Childhood And Adult Rejection And Abandonment

REJECTION HAD A STRONGHOLD ON ME WITH THE PURPOSE OF annihilating my identity in God. Rejection almost destroyed me. Early on in my childhood years, rejection kept me in bondage, not knowing who I was and not knowing how to love and embrace myself. The only time I felt deemed worthy was in the eyes of other people's perceptions of me. I lived my life needing approval from men because of the need to be accepted and to fit in. Growing up I never fit in. No matter what my status was, the cliques did not work for me.

My father's absence affected every other relationship in my life. I was very withdrawn and wasn't really open to getting to know people. I had dealt with so much betrayal that I really couldn't trust a lot of people. Instead of realizing and facing that reality, I hid behind rejection.

I dealt with rejection so much at such an early age that I embraced it without knowing it. The older I got the more I became guarded and awkward in environments. I didn't know how to trust and who to trust. I couldn't be myself with unfamiliar people, only with the people who truly knew me. I remember to this day my pastor telling me at the age of 18 years old that God had placed a calling on my life, but in order for me to really fully walk in that calling I had to be willing to overcome men's opinions of me. It was very hard.

The spirit of rejection paralyzed me for years. Rejection showed up in every area of my life: my connections, workplace, ministry, and even in my relationships. There were moments I felt like I was delivered and set free from this spirit, until something happened to remind me that I wasn't free. It was a recurring cycle. I struggled with self-rejection and self-sabotaging. I began to sabotage my own life by rejecting myself and not accepting who God called me to be. I began to pass up opportunities of open doors and embracing my true authentic self.

From the moment I was conceived, I had to endure the outcome of my parents' broken relationship and the things that occurred even before I was born. Feeling abandoned and unloved growing up, I camouflaged rejection very well. Oftentimes I told people that I was an introvert, which I was, but my reasoning for not connecting with others was because I was hiding behind rejection. I continued to isolate myself from people because of fear of being hurt, betrayed, or deceived.

I was so used to being rejected that I felt like I needed to be accepted. Rejection is not a good feeling. It hinders you and affects your whole life. Rejection was something that I dealt with for many years. I remember at the age of 23 when God so plainly told me to turn to a Bible scripture. It was Galatians 1:10 which says, "For do I now persuade men, or God? or do I seek to please men? for if I yet pleased men, I should not be the servant of Christ." That scripture really hit me. At that moment I realized that I'm not here to please men, but I'm here to please God. At the end of the day, when you become secure in who you are in God, it doesn't matter who approves you or not. However, even after that moment I still battled depression so badly that I didn't know how to break the spirit. I was in bondage to depression when I was in bondage to rejection.

CHAPTER 10

Generational Curses

I REMEMBER THE PERPETUAL, UNHEALTHY BEHAVIORAL PATTERNS IN MY life. Some of those unhealthy habits and behaviors that started in my childhood helped shape me into an adult. Some cycles were deeply rooted before I was even born.

My family was chosen by God, but struggled with generational alcohol abuse, and other sins like backbiting, harsh talk, animosity, jealousy, and disobedience, which hindered and even paralyzed us. I conformed to those same patterns growing up, until God began to reveal to me the unhealthy patterns that I had adopted in my own life.

My family members were fighters. Fighting was part of the culture that I grew up in. If you mentioned our last name we were judged right away. I was caught up in that same nature. Even after giving my life to Christ, people continued to have the wrong perception of who I was because of my past. Fighting was the only time we were able to come together as a family, besides when the matriarch and rock of our family, my grandma, brought us together.

For many years I wondered why I struggled with things and continually went on a rant. Not knowing that there were demonic influences and open doors that kept me from moving forward, sometimes these influences affected my behavior. I would get so close towards my breakthrough just to find myself in the same cycles. Those perpetual cycles were because of generational curses and ancient ruins that happened before I existed and were rooted in my bloodline. Growing up I got caught up in worldly systems that were not Godly, but they were traditional things that were taught and deemed to be the normal way of life. As children, it is only natural that you adapt to your environment. What you teach children and expose them to have the potential to produce good or bad fruit.

Growing up I knew there was something unique about my family and that we were chosen by God. My grandma was a pastor and my grandfather was in the Mason cult. There were always struggles because of generational sins. Even with the powerful mantle that was on my grandma's life and the pouring out of the oil, some still turned deaf ears to the biblical teachings. For many years our family did not understand that "many are called but few are chosen" to do the will of God.

I remember as a young woman in my early twenties going to church, I would pray and fast concerning my family and the ancient ruins and generational curses. One of the generational curses was alcohol abuse. When I asked my mother how her father passed she said it pertained to alcohol abuse. I had an uncle that died from alcohol abuse as well. I began to see how alcohol shaped the dynamics of our family. When a family member was intoxicated, anger and rage took over, which led to unhealthy conversations that ended up in fights. I saw the difference between when some family members were sober and when they started drinking. Once the alcohol was in their system their behavior changed. I saw a lot of dysfunctional behavior that had the potential to affect my family. However, I know that one day God will deliver my family and myself from ungodly cycles.

CHAPTER 11

Struggling With My confidence

FOR AS LONG AS I COULD REMEMBER I STRUGGLED WITH CONFIDENCE. Growing up oftentimes I felt inadequate and not good enough. I struggled with believing in who God said I was because slander, curse words, and manipulative behavior were considered normal in my family. After many life disappointments and failures, I realized having the wrong mindset was hindering my life. I realized that I was what I believed. The mind is powerful, so my thoughts became my reality. I started to operate in a place of mediocrity. As soon as doubt came, I felt that I did not have what it took to accomplish or see things to the end. Even as a child I did not feel good enough to participate in school activities. I remember getting picked to be on the drill team and feeling like I didn't have the looks or I wasn't the best dancer. So, I dropped out of the drill team. At that moment I got used to hiding in the shadows. Because of my own insecurities, I was okay if no one noticed me.

I had a one-on-one interview with one of the Human Resource managers and it did not go well at all. My lack of confidence showed up in my interview. My interviewer turned around and told me "You lack confidence. This is a major disadvantage because you are definitely qualified for the position. You dressed the part and your resume is very impressive, yet you don't believe in yourself." I was so disappointed and embarrassed, but I took the constructive criticism and grew from it. I felt this was a lesson that pivoted me in the right direction for growth.

One of the struggles that I was embarrassed about and that I had to learn to embrace was that I had a speech impediment and was so uncomfortable with speaking in public. The speech impediment was passed down from my mother, and out of all four of my mother's children, I was the only child that had it. I now believe it was only so bad because I made it bigger than what it was. Sometimes my speech impediment caused me to shut down in the middle of conversations. Usually, I would blurt out dorky words to take away from the embarrassment, and sometimes I wasn't taken seriously. However, I was reminded about how God's grace is sufficient for me. God did not allow my speech to block his divine plans for my life. With the many assignments that God has called me to, I had the pleasure of speaking on multiple platforms without expertise, but with the Holy Spirit's impartation. God's plans outweigh all opposition and imperfections, and his divine power is limitless.

At first I did not realize that God created us all to be unique and to be set aside, and that I should embrace the beauty of the gifts he placed inside of me to fulfill his purpose on earth. I remember admiring influential leaders that spoke so clearly and were sure of who they were and who they were called to be. I later realized that God was preparing and positioning me to also be an influential leader. My freshman year in college I took public speaking and I literally had to face my fears. But when it came to confidence oftentimes it had a lot to do with my environments. In some environments I would thrive, and in others I would struggle. I give all glory to God because, although I was nervous in my class, I passed it with a high B. I realized that God made me different and that I thrive with a lot of visual aids. So, God gave me a strategy that helped me get over my fear and anxiety. I did all of my presentations with a projector and objects, and I was literally able to flow.

I learned not to self-sabotage myself but to retrain my thought patterns. Every day I had to talk to myself like someone that I love. There was a great level of reprogramming happening inside of me. I was worth the life that God had promised me, so I shut the door to my insecurities. I was no longer walking in imposter syndrome, but I was believing that the doors God had opened for me were for me. I was stepping out of my comfort zone, and God was repositioning me for something greater.

As a woman that continues to grow in God, I now realize that God regards the people that we consider misfits. In fact, God has the power to beautify them and use them to bring glory to his name. Therefore, I don't have to walk around feeling incomplete. I have learned that I am fulfilled in Christ Jesus.

CHAPTER 12

Seeking For Wholeness In Relationships

I REMEMBER A TIME WHEN I DID NOT HAVE THE BEST RELATIONSHIP with my parents. Since I grew up in a single parent home with my mother, I did not have that emotional bond with my father. I sought approval from people because I felt I was different from my family and peers. It was really hard for me, and so I was searching for a love that was real. But how could I identify real love when I had not seen real authentic connections?

My mother was there, but I felt like she did not understand me. The things that I had experienced had already helped to shape who I was. My mother raised me with what she had. Whatever tools she used kept me clothed, fed, and clean. But among those great necessities was a hurt little girl. There were some unhealthy cycles that were passed down to me. Our family dynamics caused unhealthy boundaries, frustration, and built-up anger. However, we were taught to keep going on with life as usual and that family must stick together, no matter what. As a result, unresolved issues continued to brew in the family, and it caused unforgiveness to set in.

As a resilient woman, Mom carried the hurt of her children. Even as a single parent, she never stopped praying for all of us. No matter what we were going through, she seemed to always keep things together the best way she knew how. Because my mother was a single parent, as the oldest child, I sometimes had to act as the second mother in the household.

My mother was an unhealed woman who had been through a lot in her own personal life. However, being busy with parenting really made it almost impossible to tend to her own mental health. She was always putting her life on hold to serve others. Because my mother was big on forgiveness, oftentimes she would put up with a lot of toxic behavior from people. Her belief was that God would handle everything. She didn't realize that God gives us the wisdom to separate ourselves from things and people that are not healthy for our lives. However, Mom believed that she had to put up with certain toxic and dysfunctional behaviors in her life. I never understood how she was able to handle people with so much grace, always available to pray, undergird, and support them, especially family. Oftentimes she played caregiver roles to family members who really despised her. So growing up, I learned to walk that same path. I felt the burden to help and be responsible for other people's problems.

I became a caregiver as a teenager. At 15 years old, I took on this role not really able to be a teen. Young caregivers, like myself, sometimes take on adult roles because we feel pressured to take on others' responsibilities. Without a male role model in the household, as the older sibling, sometimes I had to pick up the slack and be accessible and available to the needs of the immediate and extended family.

Sometimes my mother was my biggest cheerleader, and other times I felt like she was too hard on me. I remember searching for a relationship with my father because I felt like I was so different and misunderstood by my immediate family. I wanted to know who I was and be able to identify myself among my family.

As a teenager, I longed for wholeness in relationships and friendships. So, I started hanging around the wrong group of friends who were getting in trouble for stealing from malls and department stores, which was getting me in trouble with my mom. She disliked the negative impact that some of my friends had on me. I thought everyone was my friend not even realizing that I was in toxic relationships and friendships. I really felt like my life sucked, and I did not understand why. I was lost and angry. I felt alone and longed for love, even if I was being loved incorrectly. My mother tried to shield me from a lot of life's hurts and disappointments. I did not know at the moment, but I was self-destructing.

Later, I wanted my mother to understand that those unhealthy, generational cycles had brought emotional distress and trauma to my siblings and me. The best way to protect her children was to get rid of those unhealthy cycles and create healthy, godly cycles.

CHAPTER 13

Delayed But Not Denied

A FTER BEING FRUSTRATED WITH SOME OF MY LIFE DECISIONS, I decided to make the best out of my situation. One day I had a conversation with my mom about my future plans. I realized that I wasn't alone anymore, but I had a child who was depending on me for everything. The pressure of being a good mom was weighing on me. I wanted my son to have better opportunities in life. So, I started praying more and declaring the word of the Lord over my son's life. I prayed for God to bless him with a really loving consistent male figure in his life that would help and assist in the right direction.

God did just that and blessed my son, at the age of three, with a very dope guy. One day while I was at a temp service, I connected with a guy from my childhood, James, and we started going out on dates. One day he asked to take our relationship to the next level. James was extremely active in my son's life. He supported, and provided for my son and did everything with him. Around that same time, my son's biological dad and I started really communicating better for the sake of our son.

The following year I started looking into enrolling in The Ohio State University, but my grandma suggested that leaving my son at such a young age was not a good idea. So, I decided to stay in the city and go to Cincinnati State, a community college that was only 12 minutes away from my house. I majored in Physiology, but I still could not decide what I wanted to do. I ended up wasting a year in school in a field that had nothing to do with what I really had a passion for. I remember sitting in my bedroom and thinking about what I really wanted to do. The only thought that came to my mind was fashion, and all of a sudden, I got excited! I thought to myself, "I want to be a boutique owner and fashion designer." I took a trip down memory lane thinking about how I would go to church and receive the same prophetic word that I was going to be a fashion designer. It seemed like that was the prophetic word I got every time I got a word. I thought, "Why are y'all in my head?" I then chuckled to myself because every time my mom would buy me an outfit, I would revamp it. So, it all started to make sense. Later I went to my college guidance counselor and told her that I wanted to change my major. When she asked me if I was sure, I said, "Yes, business is what I want to do." Afterwards I prepared for school and bought everything that I needed: laptop, Microsoft word, desk, etc.

I also continued looking for another job. I got a call for an interview and got hired right away. I put a two weeks' notice in at White Castle and started at Montgomery Inn as a tray carrier. At the time that new job worked better for me because in the fall I was starting college. When school started, I was taking all advanced classes except for math. Ever since junior high school, I always struggled in math and I always wanted to just get by. But now I was faced with some major academic challenges that I realized I could not overlook. I got a tutor right away. The tutors were awesome because I saw my knowledge enhancing. As a young mother, I was dedicated to evolving so that I could give my son a better life and be a role model for him, as well as for other people. As I progressed and moved on to my core classes, because I had grown up fast, I became a little distracted.

Having missed out on my childhood, sometimes I desired to just be a young teen girl, but I also understood that I was a teen parent growing into a young adult and there were limitations to my lifestyle. Sometimes I would hang out with my female cousins and go to parties whenever I could ask my mom to babysit. As a parent, life was lonely, and I did not have the kind of freedom that I was used to. Being a young parent wasn't easy at all. I had to deal with a son who had come home on oxygen. Between work and school, I needed a little break, not realizing that as a mother, there were no breaks. I lost a lot of friends because I was a young parent. Every decision was based on my son's well-being.

Although having a child did not heal me from past traumas, at the time, it helped ease the pain. Since I still had not fully healed, I started going to parties, smoking and drinking. Gin was my favorite liquor. Every day I felt unloved and unwanted, and I did not know the meaning of self-love. So, I covered up by smoking weed and Black & Mild cigars and drinking alcohol, until one day when I just laid in bed feeling hopeless. In that moment, I prayed for God to come in and help me with all the bitterness. That day I did not have the desire to party, smoke and drink. I realized I had been living my life in sin.

Shortly after I lost my uncle Dan who had been a consistent male role model to me as a child growing up. Although I was grieving, I tried to capture those positive memories in my mind, like when he was teaching me how to drive through the parking lot and how he chuckled because he noticed how nervous, yet determined I was. There were so many more memories I will never forget.

I remember hanging out, going to parties, shopping at the mall, and having fun with one of my favorite cousins Sheena. As I continued to work and go to college trying to create a different life for my son, my cousin was struggling with substance abuse trying to hide from the pain of abandonment and rejection that she was experiencing. I was a listening ear and a support system for her as much as I could. One day she called and told me about a dream she had. She dreamed of losing her life on her birthday. Shortly after she lost her life. When I found out I broke down and I couldn't stop crying.

At that point, I realized all of the unexplainable losses were extremely hard on me. I remember not being able to function at all. I was grieving so badly that when I visited a church where my grandma was preaching, a prophet told me to stop grieving or it would take me out prematurely. But even after that, I was still not able to function in school because my heart was aching so badly. I would just stare at the computer screen in school. My instructor came to me in private and asked me if I was okay. I told her what happened as I began to break down in tears. My teacher and I agreed that I should take some time off from school. I took the term off and tried to collect my thoughts. I remember hugging my son tightly because I felt like death was close to home. The pain eventually became a little easier to overcome.

Later, I reconnected with my childhood crush James at work. His mom and I worked for the same company. When he picked her up on Valentine's Day, he brought her a dozen roses. At first he glanced at me, and then he stared at me more like he was trying to figure out who I was. His mom smiled and said, "I remember you when you were a child." As I reached over and hugged her, he mentioned to me that he had a vision when he was a child that I was going to be his wife. So, we talked briefly, exchanged numbers and started dating shortly after that. It seemed like everything happened so fast. Many nights he cried with me about the losses and trauma that I experienced. I realized that he clung to me quickly because, for some reason, I was that missing piece in his life. We came from two different backgrounds, but we were both able to relate to hurt. We dated for three years and broke up. I wanted more out of the relationship besides boyfriend and girlfriend status. I came from a different moral background. I wanted to be a wife and build with a husband that was willing to lead. So, we broke up and I went back to school at a private college to finish and get my degree.

CHAPTER 14

A Young Woman Thriving

AFTER TAKING A SABBATICAL FROM COLLEGE TO ALLOW MYSELF TO grieve, I just wanted life to be back to normal. The loss that I had experienced within that year had taken a toll on me and my heart. Losing loved ones and friends is not easy, but I had to continue to live. I did not realize at that time that death is part of life. I was still just trying to process everything. However, my past or the recent loss did not deter me from my future. It slowed down the process, but it did not stop me from progressing in life. After my son's asthma was under control, I began planning for a better future. My life started looking up. I was more optimistic about my future plans.

As a child growing up, I always felt that there was more to life. Oftentimes, I felt like I was misunderstood by people. I was called bougie or accused of thinking I was better than everyone. I remember going to family barbecues and being criticized instead of embraced. I was told by a cousin, "I always felt like you thought you were better than us." That made me uncomfortable to be around my family. I never felt I was better, but I wanted better. God was using me to break generational cycles and barriers in the family. My children were also prejudged because their father and I placed moral values in them.

The fact that I wanted more out of life caused controversy amongst the people I loved. My own immediate family did not understand me, but my mother always surrounded me with some trailblazing women, such as my grandma who wore many hats. She was a great influence in my life and taught and inspired me to be a Godly woman. If anyone knew, it was my grandma. She saw the witty ideas and creativity that God placed inside of me. And my mentor Sharon, who was a woman with beauty and brains, inspired me not to be only a pretty face, but an educated woman. This sometimes caused tension in my household and amongst my family. I felt penalized for wanting more out of life instead of living a life where I had to settle. I became what I was exposed to. For instance, college had always been a part of my plans growing up. I wanted to do something great in life, and provide a better life for my family.

When I decided to go back to school I enrolled in a private college with a double major. Instead of just applying to get an Associate's degree in Business, I majored in Business Administration & Management so I could learn how to manage and gain knowledgeable skills about the operational functions in the office. At this point of life, I was proud of how far I had come and the milestone God allowed me to reach. While working and going to school, I saved up enough money to get my own apartment. I was so excited.

Although my mom and I were not always on the same page, I wanted to grow and learn what life was all about. With the right guidance from my mother and the right support from my grandma, I learned a lot about saving money, sacrificing and putting money away. My first apartment was in the Fay Apartments. I was so glad to finally be on my own. That same week I got all my furniture moved to my new apartment except for my living room furniture which came that next week. I was living and grateful to be out on my own. Somehow I let my ex-boyfriend move in with me a month after I got my own apartment, and I was always feeling convicted because I really didn't believe in shacking up. I believed in marriage first. My grandma always told me, "Why pay for the cow if you get the milk for free." My morals and values wouldn't allow me to continue shacking up for long.

I remember feeling so convicted because I was reading and learning more about God's word. Getting connected to God was important to me. I learned that sometimes while you are young in a relationship, you think you have the relationship thing figured out, but in reality, you are teaching each other as you go along and still getting to know who you are. I asked myself, "Who are you? What's your purpose in life?" Although I wasn't a PK (a pastor's kid), you would have thought I was because I was very careful about my decisions. As a young woman, I just wanted to please God. So, one day I sat down after dinner and told my boyfriend at the time that I no longer wanted to live in sin. While tears were rolling from my eyes, it was the hardest thing to tell him that we could no longer live together. He was disappointed with me making this decision while we were a year steady in the relationship.

Once we moved out, we started spending less time with each other, and before I knew it, he would only pick me up to take me to and fro, and to spend time with my son. He had been in my son's life since he was 3 years old and I did not want to take that away from my son. He gave my son consistency that, at the time, his biological father could not give him. So, we formed a co-parent relationship and I moved on with my life.

While living in the projects, it became so violent that I used to pray every day that God would keep me and my son and bless us with something better. Every other day I heard gunshots on the regular. When I tell you that God will not put more on you than you can bear, I mean it. One day there was a shootout behind my son's back window. I brought my son into my bedroom and began thanking God for his protection. I called my mom and told her what was going on and she picked him up the next day. When I went in the backyard to bring in the grill, I saw a bullet shell by my son's back window and started rejoicing because I learned at that moment that God is a keeper. The following week I got a call from a really upscale apartment complex that was patrolled by the police. I was so glad to move from that location. I was closer to school and my mom could help take my son to school. My environment was safer and I had peace. I was able to throw dinner parties and just enjoy life.

My testimony is how God transformed my life. I started going to another church and my overseer Prophetess Rose, at that time, was very influential in my life and would speak into my life. She was a seeing prophet and a lot of my gifts were activated in her ministry. Many prophetic words she spoke into my life have come to pass. I was a firm believer but I didn't have the Holy Spirit. Not only was Prophetess Rose my spiritual leader, but she became my spiritual mother and my mentor. I learned so much from her and the godly wisdom that came out of her mouth. She assisted me in ministry, marriage, family, and there was a powerful impartation she imparted in my life.

My pastor used to call me just to check on me. One day we had a powerful conversation and she said she would pick me up on Sunday for church. When I went to church that Sunday I felt like I needed to rededicate my life to God. There was something so different about my encounter with God this time. My relationship with God was now personal and not based on my family's relationship with God.

I was really learning and growing in God, but I still had some fear from my past memories. For instance around 12 years of age, I felt insecure and rejected by God because I witnessed other children shouting and speaking in tongues in church during a tarrying service. There was one girl in particular that would tease me really bad. She told me, "If you do not shout right now, you are going to hell." I did not shout like the other children, and I felt again the pain and rejection that I felt being rejected by my absent father. This hindered me from even connecting to God on a closer level, and at one point I thought God did not love me. But, the more I got to know God the more I realized that God can use me however he chooses. I removed the limitations off of God. I remember my leader and spiritual mom at the time told me, "Don't let what seems so grand make you feel insignificant to God. Sometimes you're closer to God than you think." I remember that day the feelings of value and acceptance filled my heart. I was a young adult and realized it's time when God says it's time! I remember sometimes we had service three times a week: Sunday, Wednesday, and Friday.

One night during a Friday service, the presence of God was high. My spiritual mother came to me and told me, "God said it's time to receive his precious gift of the Holy Ghost." That night I got it! The power of God was on me so heavy as I began to speak in tongues. I was told I shouted all over the church. It happened at God's appointed time during that Friday night service.

The power of God was all over me that night, and when I came home, I was still praising God in the tub. My mom, who wasn't in church at the time, heard me from downstairs. All I know is that God's presence reigned all through my mom's house and interrupted her plans. That night Mom stopped partying and started praising God. She fully surrendered her life back to Christ. The next day my mother told me she was delivered and had rededicated her life to Christ. God used me as a vessel that night. As she heard me praising, she received instant deliverance.

After I received the Holy Ghost, I had a hunger and thirst for God like never before. While my son was at school I would pray and read my word for hours. However, although I had a God that loved me, I was still struggling with life trauma, and pain. I still felt I wasn't good enough because of past hurt, rejection and abandonment issues. I remember going to my spiritual mother and she would pray for me, and I felt so encouraged and full of hope. I continued to surround myself with the saints so that I could be strengthened. Being a Christian on just spiritual milk, it was so easy to go back out there in the world. So, I stayed in my word and prayed for God's grace. However, it seems like every time you are focused and avoiding distractions, the enemy comes with a new trick. I lost friends because they did not understand that I was marked by Christ and I no longer owned my life. A lot of my family did not embrace the saved, sanctified, and Holy Ghost filled woman I had become. I was new and transformed. So, I remember being so lonely and just hanging around seasoned saints or older women to get a little godly wisdom.

CHAPTER 15

My Personal And Intimate Relationship With God

IVING MY LIFE TO CHRIST FOR MYSELF WAS THE BEST DECISION I HAVE ever made. I began to seek God even more. My new life cost me my old life. I had to give up some old friends, relationships, and environments. I grew up in an era where being saved felt like you had to almost be perfect. As a teenager and young adult, I remember beating myself up because I felt as though I wasn't allowed to be human and make mistakes. The more I grew in God the more I realized that I had the benefit of knowing God for myself. I was attending a powerful prophetic ministry and I was blessed to have a prophetic pastor who had a powerful prophetic mantle on her life. I remember the signs, miracles and demonstration of God's power in the church services. My spiritual mother told me, "Don't lose your seasoning." I did not understand it then, but as I got older I understood how important it is to stay seasoned for God, not lose my zeal for God and not compromise the word. I continued to study and stay rooted and grounded in the Lord so that I could grow from spiritual milk to spiritual meat. I began to spend more personal time with God reading my word, praying, and learning the power behind fasting.

I was changing for the good and I was happy about it. Sometimes I had to miss out on parties because I was at Friday night church services. I was really busy learning more and staying under the anointing and the word of God. As a young woman, I used to fast a lot and read the word of God for hours, allowing God to illuminate his word to me. Spending time with God made my painful trauma seem small. I was able to cry out to him sometimes not having words to say, but knowing that the Holy Spirit was making intercession for me.

Everything about my life changed, even my taste in men. In the past it seemed like I was attracted to bad boys, even though my morals and values were different from my attraction. But now I was dating a young Christian man. We went out to nice restaurants and to the movies, just enjoying life. We dated for about six months and then went our separate ways. I wasn't fully ready to let my guard down. I feared abandonment that happened in my past from my dad. I hadn't overcome that kind of trauma yet, so I couldn't trust a man. It seemed like everywhere I was dealing with the same cycle but in a different package.

I remember spending time with God and encountering him in a mighty way. I was hearing God's voice and watching him defend me from my enemies. While going to college at Cincinnati State door after door was opening up for me. God was all in my life. Prayer was definitely vital and a powerful tool in my life. Although I was growing closer to God, I still wanted to fill that void in my life. I wanted fulfillment from a relationship because I felt lonely. I desired to be loved as a young woman, but in a healthy way. So, I dodged temptation for as long as I could until my past crept up.

CHAPTER 16

Breaking Free From Unhealthy Relationships

THE TOXIC AND ABUSIVE BEHAVIORS THAT I HAD EXPERIENCED IN LIFE set the tone for what I would allow to be my standard in relationships for years. Starting at an early age, I was in unhealthy relationships where I was dealing with physical and verbal abuse. For instance, when I was around 17 years old, I was trying to run away from the life that I could not seem to heal from. I was in a relationship that lasted for almost 2 years, but because of wrong motives and lies, I called off the engagement. This decision caused my ex-fiancé to become angry. Shortly after stalking me for months, he threatened me in public. I remember a male friend of mine was in the same area at the time. When he looked at me he knew something was wrong and he asked me, "Love is everything okay?" This was enough to make my ex back off. That day my friend saved my life. The fear of what could have happened didn't happen. God intervened on my behalf and I thanked him for his divine protection. After that, I prayed that God would please allow my ex-fiance to fall in love with someone else so that I could move forward. God really heard my prayers and my ex left me alone for good and I haven't heard from him again. The harassment and stalking stopped completely. I then took a break from relationships and started focusing on me.

As soon as I moved forward and got focused, I ran into my childhood crush James. We started casually dating, not getting too serious. Before I knew it, I found myself falling back in love again. He continued to pursue me, but one day he got in trouble with the law and had to go to jail. Later on, he asked me to marry him. I thought he was joking because clearly, I felt like he was not ready for such a serious commitment. Once he got out, we started dating again.

I was now going to a new ministry because my spiritual mother no longer had her church. The bishop at my new ministry pressured us to marry too soon. I was a young woman that hated to displease God so I went along with the plan not really consulting God first. The leadership wasn't concerned about us having a successful marriage. Although we both weren't really prepared, one day my bishop called me and said, "Y'all need to get married now. The bible says it's better to marry than to burn." With much manipulation I fell into the trap and agreed to get married right away. Yes, we loved each other, but love alone won't keep a marriage together. We were unprepared. But she really did not consider that we did not have all the necessary tools for a successful marriage.

I received a call one day, "Get ready! I am on my way there to marry y'all."

I replied, "I don't even have anything to wear."

"Well, find something!"

I was a young woman and felt pressured, so I agreed.Our parents did not approve of our decision, but we felt like we were in love and ready, so I got married at the age of 23 years old. Because of the era I was in at the time, marriage was extremely important. Even though we got counseling, the timing was off. My church was looking out for their image and did not understand that we weren't mature enough for marriage. In my church, you were looked down on if you were having ongoing causal relations without the goal of marriage. So, on October 9, 2005, I got married because I was in love and afraid to be alone. I wanted to feel whole, loved and fulfilled.

The same week when we got married, I was lying next to my husband in bed and I started having multiple dreams, sometimes in one night, of different women of different nationalities. I prayed and asked God, "What is going on Lord? What is it?" And the next day I had the same dreams again. I cried to God because I knew doing things on my own accord was going to cost me something. At the age of 23, I was stressed, and I felt like it was too early to be already struggling with our marriage and dealing with trust issues. James wasn't fully mature for marriage. I had to learn how to adapt to my new lifestyle as a wife. We were a young married couple that did not have the right people to pour into us. There was a lot of trial and error. We were learning more about who we were as individuals. We began to have a lot of petty arguments that led to some physical altercations.

I remember the petty disagreements that we used to have. Three months into the marriage I found out that I was pregnant. I was so happy and he was too because this was his first baby. I felt like a child would bring us closer but it didn't. Stress from the inside and outside influences put a strain on our marriage. I was pregnant and frustrations were high because he was not there which made the arguments more intense. I remember thinking that our marriage was toxic. In front of people, I was hiding behind makeup while hurting inside. During my whole pregnancy, I was so sick. My doctor made me go on early bedrest because of pregnancy complications. I had to stop working and take a leave of absence from school.

We were in a rough patch. We were young, married, dealing with financial problems, and not having everything figured out. Our family was expanding and now I was pregnant. I was so depressed about being pregnant. Being unequally yoked caused friction in our household. Because of the pregnancy, the enemy was running rampant in my mind. He would tell me negative things about the baby, and I was crying a lot. I never felt so imbalanced and unable to take control of my life and emotions.

Even though my emotions were all over the place, when I went to the doctor and found out I was having a girl, I got excited! So, I tried to get into the swing of things. One thing I knew for sure was the power of prayer. I surrounded myself with people who were praying and undergirding me while I was going through it.

As a babe in Christ, I needed a sense of hope and encouragement. One Sunday I went to church and we had a guest speaker who unexpectedly called me up, prayed, and prophesied to me. "You don't feel too good about the baby that you are carrying."

I replied, "I don't know."

She said, "The baby that you are carrying is going to be a powerful leader in God. You don't know what you are carrying. Protect her. Teach her about God. She will be reading the bible at an early age. Continue to protect her."

I began weeping because I had struggled every day being sick and depressed throughout my whole pregnancy. I went from allowing the pain that I was experiencing to consume me to shifting my mindset and finding hope in Christ Jesus. I started praying for my baby and reading the bible to her while she was in my womb. I realized at this point that I was carrying a gift from God.

I remember getting so huge with this pregnancy that I started walking close to my due date. Towards the end of August, a beautiful girl was born at 7 pounds and 6 ounces. She was the most beautiful little baby I had ever seen. Within two weeks, my body was bouncing back, I was driving and I was ready to start back to school and work. Even though the finances were not like I wanted them to be, my first daughter had everything that she needed and more. Her dad bought her almost everything and I was so grateful.

After having my baby girl, the next month, I was getting sick from everything. I did not think anything of it until I started to get a little bulge in my stomach. One day I was at my mother's house and she said, "Love, you are pregnant." Not knowing, I denied it. The following week I went to the doctor and found out I was pregnant again. I was so hurt because I had to adjust my life around my second baby. I started dealing with postpartum stress disorder even more. I had constant mood swings and oftentimes I felt like I did not want the pregnancy. I started dealing with so many problems in my marriage and I knew another child was not going to help the situation. We had separated after having my first daughter, and I had fearful thoughts that the baby I was carrying wasn't going to make it. My husband wanted a boy, but I wanted another girl. When I went to the doctor, I found out I was having a girl. He was a little disappointed because we were having another girl, but then he became excited. With my last baby girl I had a C-section and she was taken out on the same day of my middle child's birthday, giving them the same birthday.

Although my husband and I were separated, we got back together. The whole time we were separated there was infidelity going on in the marriage. We tried to stay together to make it work for the children, but somehow, we couldn't seem to reconcile, so I filed for a divorce. I wanted to show my children what a healthy godly relationship looks like and that they are to be treated with respect.

One day my ex-husband and I had a talk and decided once again to bring the family back together for the sake of the children. It seemed to work for a while but eventually we grew apart. We had played the makeup and break up game so many times that it did more harm to our children. I desired consistency and an image that my children could model after.

I sat down and talked to God. I asked him about my future and moving forward as a single parent. Being single was such a difficult transition, but I was ready for change. Telling our children was going to be very hard. But I remembered that I had a mandate. I told myself, "If we aren't moving forward and growing together, then I have to move forward." As the woman I was becoming, I knew my worth. I sat my children down one day. I believe my son Dontae was 11, my middle daughter Reny was 5 and my youngest daughter Taylor was 4 years of age. I told them, "You know Dad and I love each other, right?" They said yes. I then said, "We are no longer together, but we will continue to co-parent." I remember the look on my baby's face of disappointment and fear.

Every day I witnessed my children's brokenness during the divorce process. Even after the divorce, my middle daughter would stare out the window every day to see if her daddy was coming back home. I had to witness and experience the instant change, tears, and hurt from my children. It seemed like my middle child Reny had the hardest time adjusting after the divorce. One day she came running to me crying and asking, "Mommy is it my fault that you and Daddy are divorcing? Did I do something wrong?" I told her no and that we loved her so much. But what do you say to a 5-year-old that is experiencing this type of pain? As a parent, naturally, I wanted to protect my children from every little boo boo or pain they experienced. But the fact was that I could not heal the pain that they were experiencing. Only God and time could heal those painful wounds.

When the divorce was filed it seemed like I went through several stages in the process. In the first stage, I was so happy to get out of such a toxic relationship. In the second stage, I started missing the family-like environment that came from our 11 years of history. In the third stage, I realized that the decision was necessary and it was time for me to put an end to this cycle. The real pain continued at home in the bed where I cried tears of hurt and betrayal.

When I went to court, he did not show up because he did not want to grant me my divorce. I prayed to God for answers and for the decisions that he has planned for my life. I got to a place where my desire was to obey God. God instructed me to let that toxic marriage go. So, I finally went to court and my lawyer granted my divorce and the terms that I asked for. My ex-husband and I came up with an agreement for our children in order to move forward, and we figured out how we were going to work out our co-parenting plans

I remember my home girls asking me if I was okay and me replying yes when I was still hurting. Although I wanted the divorce and was ready to move on with my life, I still loved my ex-husband deeply and I knew I couldn't just erase the time and love that we shared.

At the beginning stage of my healing process, I started to miss what I once had. During the last stage of the process, I was learning how to release what was and focus on what is. I remember that last release came with extreme weeping. I saturated my pillows with tears day in and day out, but nights were the worst. I really had to cry out to God to help me get over this pain. God did just that. I had to divorce my ex-husband out of my spirit and be released from the soul ties. Day-by-day things became easier for me and I was able to live life. God restored and rebuilt me as a woman allowing me to see how valuable I am in God. I understood my life did not end but I was embarking on a new journey. I began to feel okay even when I wasn't fully healed from the breakup because of our children. I started to take self-love moments for myself like taking trips and doing something nice for myself. I remember one day cutting my hair short and dying it. I wanted a new me because I was starting completely over.

After the divorce we matured and became really good friends. At one point we even felt we were going to remarry, but I didn't want to give in to my emotions. We just continued to do what was best for our children. Co-parenting became important in our parental agreement as parents. For instance, allowing my ex-husband's girlfriend to be a part of our children's lives wasn't an easy decision. We had to make sure their needs came first and gradually allowed her to be a part of their lives. No matter what events, birthdays, or school activities my ex and I were able to have a healthy relationship with boundaries, laughter, and respect.

CHAPTER 17

Life After Divorce

BECAUSE OF MY PAST FAILED MARRIAGE, I TOLD MYSELF THAT I DID not want to get married again. I felt like I had invested too much, and I know God is a God of order. I remember being in a relationship that wasn't ordained by God and after one night of just crying, I went to bed and dreamed of a really good God-fearing man that was going to be my husband. At that moment I was able to face tomorrow with hope because of the glimpse of my future. I had been divorced for 5 years and randomly dated, but nothing serious. I was just having fun living life.

Living the new norm, I finally got my divorce papers. I was really dealing with the fact that the man that I had spent 11 years with was finally a part of my past. After the divorce I literally had to start over with almost everything. I didn't even have a car. I left a 3-bedroom house, had a rummage sale and I got rid of all the furniture in my old house and started completely over. I started looking for a new place to stay. I came across a nice 3-bedroom townhome that was very upscale and in a decent community.

As I filled out the application, I was told that there were several people that were interested in the same townhome. I prayed and asked God to allow me to get approved for the townhome. I received a call within 3 days and was approved. I was so excited I screamed with joy and excitement! I got a trunk and moved into my new place the following week. When I moved into the place, I moved in with only our beds. Wondering how I was going to get furniture, I prayed to God about my finances and asked him to give me a better career. The next day I checked my bank account and there was $1600.00 that had been deposited into my account. I called my bank teller and asked where the money had come from, and she told me that she did not know. I was so blown away because God showed up in my life again. I realized that God had given me a supernatural deposit. In the midst of the unknown, God supplied my need. Later thereafter I began living my new life as a divorced woman and I had to prepare myself to do things without a man present.

I sat my children down and explained that the roles in the home had changed. My mother and grandma were a major support system while I was getting back to the corporate world. I was so focused on rebuilding I started working two jobs to rebuild my life and work on life goals. I needed a car, so I began to pray for a reliable vehicle and went to Fairfield. I had everything that I wanted specifically written down on paper. The bible teaches us in Habakkuk 2:2 to "write the vision and make it plain." I asked God for a newer model Impala with low miles, a car payment of 230.00 per month and no leather interior. The first car lot ran my credit and tried to put me in an older Impala with the car payment amount of 450.00 monthly. I turned down the offer, but I definitely did not give up. The next day God led me to another dealer. I remember turning into a car lot and as soon as I pulled in, I knew exactly what I was looking for. When I looked toward the cars on my left, I saw the car I had prayed for with low miles and no leather seats.

At this point, I realized that God was restoring everything I thought I had lost. I remember giving God thanks for his divine appointment. The fact that I did not have to struggle was God's purpose and plan. I was so excited about what else he had in store for me. I got a second job and my CNA certification. Soon after, my grandma's health began to decline so I began working for my grandma through an agency. That same year I enrolled in National College University to accomplish my educational goals.

My life was a journey now and all my children would see the struggles in a single-family home. I remembered receiving prophecies that I was going to finish school. I got so emotional thinking about it because I had beaten the odds and every curse that the enemy had spoken against my life. While I was in school, I was on the dean's list three times. It was an honor to be able to accomplish a major milestone in life. I remember receiving the great news that I was at the finish line. I was so excited! As a single woman, I completed my educational goals.

I remember arriving at my graduation ceremony feeling proud and accomplished. The crowd screamed from the top of their lungs saying, "Go girl! You made it!" as I walked across the stage. I received my associates degree in Business Administration & Management. Even though I was more markable after being out of college, it was a little complicated working in my field. I was offered two different career paths while I was in college, but I turned them down because, at that time, I was healing from my divorce and rebuilding my life. I continued to work in the medical field for many years after college. I really loved helping the elderly and being an impact in their lives. Although I often thought about going to nursing school, business was my true passion. However, I started working at an Internal Revenue Service processing center. I was making really good money and put my vision for business on hold. Within a year at the company, I was promoted to supervisor making three times more than I was making at entry level. I was at this company for years not really thinking about my future at this company. My income as a single parent was roughly around 4000.00 a month combining both of my jobs. I was happy because after my divorce it was easy and I was in a position to financially provide for my children without struggling.

To some extent I knew that I wanted to be married again in the future, but I didn't want to do it prematurely because of loneliness or the fear of the clock ticking. After being divorced, being in a healthy marriage was important to me. I started dating a close friend and it got pretty serious. He proposed to me and I accepted, but it turned out to be the worst decision I could have made. For instance, one of my spiritual sisters was getting married but I got to the wedding late because I had the biggest fight with my fiancé. Out of support for her I still showed up late and all. At the reception I tried to enjoy myself even in the midst of me being upset. As the music was playing and everyone was enjoying themselves, I noticed one of the deacons at the church was looking at me. He came over, spoke and asked me where my fiancé was. I told him he couldn't make it and he just looked at me and continued to listen to the music that was playing. Everyone glanced at us and noticed an undeniable chemistry between us two. The first time I noticed that he really liked me, I also knew that I had a kind of situation at home that needed to be addressed. As I left the party this nice gentleman walked me to the car. Because of the ongoing disrespect and jealous outbursts from my fiancé, shortly after I called off the engagement. My ex-fiance called me every day for a whole year, but I stayed focused. I knew that he was a distraction and that focusing on God, family, and business was important to me.

No matter what decisions I made in life I always vowed to consider how it would affect my children. My ex-husband always wanted to keep our children in healthy environments. Over the years, he stayed active in their lives no matter what was going on. As the other parent, his support was always present. On our children's birthdays he was always invited and would celebrate even once I got remarried.

CHAPTER 18

Dealing With Homelessness

HOUSING WAS ROUGH FOR ME. AS A DIVORCED WOMAN WITH THREE children, I experienced every parent's worst nightmare—not being able to financially support and provide a stable home for my children. It seemed like my whole life had been a place of stabilization, but now there was a major change to my income. The company that I worked for changed owners and the new owners made many changes that affected many employees and myself. So, the money that I was once making had been cut back. I wasn't happy about it because of the lifestyle I had at that moment. So, I continued to work both jobs, and God made sure that I had more than enough. I was a supervisor making almost $4,000.00 monthly. My income decreased tremendously to under $200.00 dollars weekly. Yet God was sustaining me. It seemed like I had more than enough to manage bills, etc.

Around 2014, my life changed even more. I had been receiving public housing assistance and, because of a minor misunderstanding, I lost it. Since my income had been cut down tremendously, I couldn't pay $1,000.00 for rent, a $300.00 monthly car note, and other expenses, not including the needs of my three children, with my income alone.

Two years later in 2016, things were still rough for me. I was depleting my bank account, paying bills, and starting over. My children and I decided to move into a house with my entire immediate family. We definitely had a conflict, but at the time it was best to be roommates until everyone could stand on their own. We moved into a house in a rough neighborhood, but the rent was reasonable. I was excited because I knew I could afford it.

After living together as roommates for a year, my sister and I were ready to go because of the conditions of the house. Everyone moved out on their own. I went back on an apartment search looking everywhere for a 3-bedroom apartment, but it was limited in availability. Typically, once people moved into a 3 bedroom they didn't move out. So, I had to downsize and started looking for 2-bedroom apartments.

After finding a really nice spacious apartment. I walked into my new apartment and I loved the atmosphere, including the hardwood floors. I was happy to have my own place again. I got a really good job at the post office just trying to get my bills caught up. When I first moved to this apartment there was a young man that stood out to me, and I did not know why he stood out.

One of my closest friends Shay and I became roommates temporarily. This living arrangement really worked out because we were a major support system to each other and our families. I really experienced the value of sisterhood. We supported each other like family. We picked up our children from school and daycare. I remember coming home from work and my best friend had cooked chicken noodle soup. I remember how she prepared that meal for everyone with so much love so that everyone could eat. At this time, I really was enjoying my apartment. It started to feel like home.

One day my baby Taylor had a dream that someone broke into my home so before that dream became a reality, I got renters insurance. I knew that my daughter had prophetic dreams, so I prayed, and I was prepared. About two weeks later I came home from work early. When I walked into my apartment, I noticed everything I had worked hard for was gone. I walked into my bedroom and my bedroom window was busted out. I hurried up and called the police and they took their precious time coming. Everything in my house was gone from TVs, DVD players, Christmas tree, food out of the refrigerator and freezer, my children's clothes, boots, my son Dontae's shoes, and game systems. I was so hurt. My daughters came home from school only to walk into a horrific situation. I remember the looks on their faces when they saw all their presents were gone. Shortly after I called their dad. told him what happened, and asked if our daughters could stay with him so that I could get my home together. I called the landlord and told them what happened, and they sent maintenance over to board up the bedroom window.

I was afraid to leave my house because I did not know when they were coming back. A police report was made and I realized that staying home was not an option. The whole day was so crazy because at that moment God showed me who broke into my apartment. There was an older lady that confirmed what God showed me. I saw the same young guy look out the window with his girl as if everything was a joke. I was heated and ready to fight. Oh yes, I was a Christian but at that moment anger got the best of me.

When my 16-year-old son came home later, multiple policemen rushed to my apartment with weapons pulled on him. I said to them, "What's going on?

My son said, "I did not do anything!"

I then said, "He is just getting home from school." I was scared.

One policeman replied, "Ma'am get back!"

I said, "He didn't do anything! He just got home from school!"

They eventually let my son go. Apparently, they were responding to a call that a young male had a weapon, but after they checked my son, they realized he did not have anything on him and had a clean record. As they were letting him go, the female cop told me to never stand in the way of police affairs. I felt like this whole day was so unreal. I knew other families that had experienced being falsely accused of acts they did not commit, but it hit home when it was my own son. I became more and more afraid for my son's life. I was a divorced mother and raising a black son was hard.

My home was broken into several more times. I remember coming home and finding my door opened and they had taken food out of my freezer once again. I called the police to make another police report. Since my apartment wasn't safe anymore, I made plans to look online for apartments. I had my children's father pick up the children from school because the safety of my children was important. I called my property manager and asked to be relocated because of the constant issues and animosity between myself and the neighbors. But the property manager wouldn't accommodate me. Frustrated, I came home for the third time to see my door open. I was so angry that I was ready to fight again. I made another police report and at this point I had to leave that side of town. I called my boyfriend, and when he came, he was upset. He held me and watched my tears fall from my eyes. A total of three police reports had been made. I knew it was time to go.

January 18, 2016, was the last day that I was ever at that apartment. I was so upset, and as a Christian, I still wanted revenge. I felt that the robbers were trying to intimidate and harass me and I wasn't able to do anything about it. I had to cry out to God and understand that vengeance is God's and not mine. I had to learn not to try to fight battles that I had no control over, which is easier said than done. I had to depend on God for the miraculous things that I asked him for, but the emotional hidden pain was still there. I was dealing with so much anger that I started really walking in anger and bitterness, and it started to show.

I was losing continuously. I put my children's Christmas items in layaway just so they could have something for Christmas. I put down a large chunk of money on their layaway. On the due date, I went to pick up my layaway and found out that someone had forged my signature, canceled my layaway and stolen the money that I worked hard for. I couldn't catch a break at this time. It was always something!

I returned my new model car because I couldn't afford the car note. I was so upset because the car was close to being paid off. I prayed about it because I was afraid to get a repossession on my credit report. I asked God to humble the heart of the dealer, and he was understanding about the situation and agreed to not report it on my credit report.

I had to deal with yet another short-term housing emergency. I allowed my son to stay at my mom's to be closer to his high school and the girls were with their father temporarily. Shortly after, they moved with me to my cousin's house. Everything was in a disarray in my life. I remember crying on a number of occasions, feeling angry, and like a failure as a mother. But I was so grateful just to have a roof over our heads.

My daughters attended Raven Elementary, not knowing that God had put my daughters in a godly atmosphere full of believers. They not only took the time to pour into my daughters, but they were stern yet encouraged them to believe in themselves as children. At the time, no one in the school knew that we were homeless. Every day when I brought my daughters to school and we walked into the office, the whole office staff was so kind. I was blessed every time and God gave me so much favor and resources.

Every time something was going on in the community, they would call me and say, "Miss Love, we have coats and a voucher for uniforms." A week before Thanksgiving I was blessed with a whole Thanksgiving meal. I was so grateful and did not remember even signing up for any resources, but the principal and the receptionist were so compassionate and generous. Within that short period of time my daughters were a part of a lot of programs. I kept them active so they didn't have to focus on the tough things. The music teacher was so dope! She was a music and drama graduate and her expertise was putting on amazing performances that my daughters were a part of. I remember one day the principal hugging me as the staff got teary eyed. I told them "Thanks for being so kind. You never know what people are going through."

We stayed for about a month at our cousin's house, but because of minor miscommunication I moved into my own house in a different neighborhood. After getting settled, my daughters and I made a visit to Raven Elementary, and the whole staff was still there. When we came into the office, I was so compelled to tell my story about how I was homeless and did not tell anyone. I also began to thank them for their love, generosity, and support towards me and my family

Soon after, the blessings came in. I remember receiving a powerful word from God concerning my life. I was going to receive double for my trouble. I learned that when you sow on good soil you will reap the harvest. Even in the midst of frustrations, there wasn't any lack in my home. God kept giving me more than enough. There was an overflow of resources and open doors that were happening for me. I received a call from the store manager where my signature had been forged. I received double like God said. So, I began to be a blessing to others who were in need. I realized you can't beat God in giving!

CHAPTER 19

Taking A Chance On Love

M Y FOCUS WAS COMPLETELY ON GOD AND FAMILY. I WAS HEALING from the multiple losses I had that had me grieving. Unexpectedly, the deacon from my church and I were getting closer. He was a little older than I was, but I was open. However, I once again put up a wall because of fear of not having a healthy marriage. He was pursuing me hard though. He would always park my car, and on Sweetest Day he parked my car and put an expensive box of candy in my truck. It seemed like every weekend at church he made it obvious that he was interested in me. My past relationship was unhealthy, toxic, verbal, and manipulative. So, when I broke it off, the deacon at my church and I became exclusive.

Since I knew him before we started dating, I realized we had to be very careful because of our past relationships. There were some red flags because he had already been married several times which made me very nervous. So, we had to be careful how we handled each other.

We kept everything confidential for a little while to maintain our personal business. One day my pastor called it out and asked if we were dating. We knew we could not lie to our pastor so we spilled the beans. He was excited for us and gave us his blessings. That summer my daughters were with their dad, so we dated the whole summer. We spent a lot of time with each other. It was fun and oftentimes, spontaneous.

One day I had a dream that he was getting married. I did not have a clue that he was going to become my husband. One day during the summer after talking to me outside, he told me, "Start planning the wedding." I was pleasantly surprised because I did love this man. Spending so much time with him was a blessing. Being in a relationship with this special guy was different and I enjoyed where we were mentally. I felt that because he was 11 years older than me, he was mature, and so some things that I dealt with in my past I didn't have to deal with. We continued to keep our relationship on the hush until one day when he made things known. He went completely above and beyond to pursue me. But, I still had my doubts during the dating process. Oftentimes I thought those doubts came from fear of giving my heart to another man after my past marriage failed. Our relationship became complicated once he proposed to me.

One night after having a good time at my mother's house for a family Christmas Eve dinner, he started playing "Meet me at the Altar" by the R&B group Jagged Edge. I had no clue what was going on. He then proposed to me and I said yes. The next day I posted the proposal on social media and all hell broke loose. Once some of the ladies in the ministry found out that we were exclusively dating, there was outrage. I was the talk of the show. It was like Oprah did not have anything on me. Apparently, there were some ladies that were really good friends of his that wanted more; maybe they were more. People were speaking harshly about me. I was so upset. It made it hard to come to church and I was sick of the confusion. The discord got so bad that one lady in particular tried to slander my name. She called my mom and told her so much negative stuff about him. At one point mom questioned me and asked me, "Do you think you want to marry a man that has all of this drama tied to him?" As I responded to defend him, she replied, "This is a woman that has somehow misunderstood their relationship." As a mother she was concerned about my well-being. Stuff became more intense and the Pastor had to step in to defuse the situation. Later on, things calmed down. We got married and started to build a new life.

CHAPTER 20

Struggling To Forgive

THERE IS POWER IN FORGIVENESS. FOR YEARS I HINDERED MY OWN life holding on to the past. There were things that no longer served me nor had a place in my life. I did not realize how my unresolved trauma had infected my life. I did not know I was harboring offenses, bitterness, and resentment in my heart. I thought I was healed but in reality, I realized that I forgave with words but ignored what was going on in my heart. Even the bible teaches a lot about forgiveness, but it is usually easier said than actually done. I found myself unpacking all of the trauma and facing the demons from my past.

Sometimes not healing from the pain and offense makes it harder to forgive. For years I held on to the things that I went through in life. Trying to navigate through trauma and pain without having the right tools to lead me towards healing oftentimes had me stuck. Yes, I was saved and had been saved for years, but I knew I needed God's help and some earthly support to heal. Unfiltered thoughts and bitterness started to brew up in me. I was still holding on the disgusting memory of getting spit on and dealing with sexual abuse in junior high by a guy because I rejected him and he couldn't handle rejection. Later on, I ran into the same guy at Richie's restaurant. My heart dropped and I rushed into the bathroom. I wasn't prepared to stand right in front of the man that not only spit on me, but sexually abused me in junior high. This painful memory still affected me majorly, and I had to learn how to heal and forgive. At that moment I thought that if I had a weapon, I would cause harm to him. At the same time, I realized that I had to rebuke that thought and allow God to deal with him. I learned that I had to accept the responsibility over my life and my feelings. I knew I had to be honest with God because he knew where I was in my healing process. He knew that I held on to that pain, hated that person and disliked myself, wondering oftentimes what I did to ask for that type of disrespectful behavior that was done against me. I knew that there was a possibility that I would never get an apology for some offenses and hurtful acts that were done to me. As a child, I started to feel like I deserved it. I did not have any self-worth at that time in my life. Oftentimes I would ask why the people that were accessible to me mishandled, betrayed, mistreated, and devalued me as a person. I wondered why people who were supposed to love me walked out of my life. I had a lot of questions with empty answers, and I realized I might never receive the answers.

The painful memories of my childhood that I wasn't healed from included not fitting in because of the unforgiveness and jealousy within the family. Can you imagine going around family members that tear you down every time you are in their presence and have nothing positive to say about the woman who brought you into the world? I wanted to run away, but where? My relationship with my father was distant. I remember one day running away in elementary school. I left school and I did not return home. I ran away to a friend's house. The enemy told me that I was unloved and that was what I believed. After thinking about all the trouble that I was in, I called my mom and my grandma came to pick me up. Grandma just loved on me, and as a child growing up, she was always my safe haven.

For the most part, I lived a life full of pain. It was a cycle, like a revolving door. Every time I turned around, I was dealing with those same painful wounds. I was tired of being in pain and I would cry out unto God because I know God heals the broken heart. The most powerful decision I decided to do was get counseling. Counseling helped me put things into perspective and learn how to live life after the pain. I learned to be okay with not getting closure from my past experiences. I had to move past the questions of why and move forward to what now? In reality I realized that all things work together for my good. No matter how I felt, I knew God was in control of my life. I was moving forward into my new life, celebrating the baby steps and making progress to heal and become who God called me to be.

CHAPTER 21

God Revealing To Me My Gifts

ROWING UP I ALWAYS KNEW THAT I WAS DIFFERENT AND UNIQUE TO God; even my gifts were unique. I remember as a little girl having a sequence of dreams and sometimes, I felt like I wasn't always asleep. Oftentimes my dreams were crystal clear and concise. As a believer there are benefits that come from being saved. I did not understand a lot because I was yet learning and growing in God.

Since I was a little girl growing up in church, I have always had this thirst and admiration for God. I wanted to get to know who God was. I enjoyed church and I fell in love with Jesus even though I didn't fully know him on an intimate level. Even as an adult, that zeal and thirst remained. Growing in faith and knowing what my gifts are and what I was anointed to do were important to me. I really didn't get caught up on the titles. I just had a heart and compassion to serve. I wanted God to be so clear about what I was called to do, even in the natural. I wanted to know my passion, position, and purpose in my everyday life.

The older I got, my dreams became so real, and I felt weird about what I was seeing in my dreams. After joining my grandma's friend's church and receiving the Holy Ghost at the age of 18 years old, it seemed from that point on that my discernment and dreams were heightened. I would oftentimes encounter God's prophetic words in my dreams. Sometimes I would dream about people's situations and oftentimes before going to church, I would see a prophecy about people in my dream. I remember dreaming about my mother. In the dream God told my mother that she was going to minister to women and teach them how to walk upright before the Lord. The next day my pastor confirmed what God had spoken to me in the dream.

One day while standing in the prayer line, my pastor told me, "You have prophetic dreams and God deals with you in the prophetic realm." Later on, God revealed I am intercessor and evangelist. I really did not understand it at first but later on I remembered being in college where I was introduced to a Caucasian lady in my class. She was a really down to earth young lady. That night I dreamed about this classmate's husband cheating on her with a 16-year-old girl. The next day when I came to class she was so distraught and hurt.

Sometimes my dreams were so clear and oftentimes I would visit biblical days in my dreams. God would always give me a powerful meaning of what was being communicated in my dreams. In the biblical dreams I saw the attire and the dirt roads, even how they traveled then. I kept hearing Tamar in my dream. I asked the Lord, "What are you saying?" Then I heard so clearly "They have my judgements, but they do not have my compassion." Once I woke up, I began to cry out unto the Lord and asked him to search my heart. I said, "I want to love like you Jesus." That morning I researched and read how God showed mercy and compassion to Tamar and other women in the bible. I was so moved by this powerful message and God showed me how to apply it to my life. So I began to pray and examine my walk with the Lord. Later on, is when God revealed that I am an Evangelist.

One day I got a reality check when God showed me who I was. I had often wondered why the warfare was so massive. It was because for so many years I was running from the calling that God had placed on my life. Even as a child, I knew that I was different. I was called to be a servant of God. Even now, I think about the many times that death passed me by.

God was revealing different spirits that I was feeling and seeing in the spirit. God was developing my gifts. Sometimes I had no clue what God had placed inside of me, but he was preparing me for intercession. I was learning about spiritual warfare, how to pray, and how to dismantle false altars and false gods. God would wake me up at night to pray against spiritual wickedness and witchcraft spirits. There were plots that God would warn me about, even in ministries, and he would equip me how to war in the spirit. Not only was I an intercessor, but God had given me the authority to come against spiritual wickedness in environments. I was also taught how to respond in love and prayer, and sometimes how to disconnect.

As I was getting older, God was teaching me to rely on his word no matter what oppositions come against me. I realized that God was my life source. God had to teach me to be quiet during frustrating seasons. Even during an exciting new business venture, God would shush me. I learned that some things do not need to be told or announced. At the appointed time God will show me when to release it. God showed me that everyone wasn't rooting for me, but he encouraged me to stay the course. Even when it seemed like what God called me to do was not thriving, he would speak to me and say, "Keep going." Some days I felt like I was deep in unknown territories. Oftentimes I would go in my prayer closet and ask God, "Show me, Lord. Take me back to the drawing board of the vision that you showed me. Lord, is this assignment up?"

For a long time, I felt like Moses in the bible because he stuttered and I too had a speech impediment. I remember thinking that God was definitely mistaken. I was a major introvert and I had a hard time speaking in front of people. I would get nervous and what I intended to say actually came out wrong. In many cases I was embarrassed and I would shut down. But God definitely has a sense of humor because at the age of 16 I had my first youth conference where I was the speaker. Later, in college I had to face my fears with a public speaking class where I really stepped outside of my comfort zone and spoke in front of an audience. God was already preparing me to evangelize and get the word of God across to a lost, hopeless, and broken nation.

After having my three children early on, I also realized that God had given them prophetic gifts. My son Dontae is a seer, dreamer and from the time that he was a baby he would have visions. One day when he was around 17 years of age, he was on his way to work when he said, "Pastor is gone, Momma." Although I knew our pastor was ill, I questioned what he meant. He said, "I saw it." Later that day, we got a call saying that our pastor had passed away. My son is a very meek and humble child. My middle daughter Reny is also a seer, and at the age of 3 years she prophesied to me after I went through a painful divorce. Reny has been seeing and hearing things as a little girl. Sometimes she was afraid and I would pray for her and ask God to remove fear from her. Even as a child, Reny was a worshiper, singer, and she loved to read her bible. My daughter would see things in people and environments that sometimes she did not understand. My youngest daughter Taylor, the baby of the family, is a dreamer and intercessor. She loves to pray. She has had prophetic dreams that have come to pass. With all my children I was very selective of what I allowed into their eye gates and ear gates. The same way God reveals to his children, the enemy also presents himself to God's children. As a mother I continue to cover my children, anoint them with holy oil and emphasize how important it is for them to have the Holy Spirit.

God also revealed to me that, as an intercessor, I am an atmosphere shifter and pillar. After coming out of consecration, God would send me on assignments. I was up a lot of late nights interceding for others. I had no clue what God was doing, but I knew I was only a vessel to be used by God. It did not matter where I was, the Lord would lead me to pray for the broken and hopeless. Also at church, as an intercessor, I would set the atmosphere inside the church. I realized that God gets all the glory for the gifts that he gave to myself and my family.

God also revealed my gifts in the natural. I was a visionary and I had a strong passion for things to come alive to its full potential. I was an incubator and mindshift coach. God had given me the gift to shift minds. That is why I had to be so cautious with what I said and did. Even with trial and error the Holy Spirit had to grow and develop me in areas that only he could do.

CHAPTER 22

2020 Perfect Vision

TAKING CARE OF YOUR MENTAL HEALTH IS VERY KEY TO BEING THE best version of yourself. 2019 was a very tough year for me. I started dealing with a massive amount of stress and frustrations. I was dealing with so much grief because of the multiple losses I experienced. I was dealing with warfare from all directions: personal, church, marriage, and work. During this time my husband was so busy that he didn't realize his wife was struggling and extremely depressed. A couple of times I said, "Baby please pray for me." Sometimes I felt like I was going to break. I'm not saying he wasn't praying for me but, I felt like the whole world was caving in on me and I began to weep all through the night. Daily I asked God to keep my mom because she was struggling with her health. I poured out so much that I felt depleted. I am an encourager by nature, and I always have been. Sometimes I will feel my friends' pain and carry their pain with them instead of giving them to God. I was an emotional wreck, and this time I was the one in need of encouragement. I started isolating myself from everyone and spending a lot of time in my bedroom with idle thoughts running through my mind. It seemed like everyone that was connected to me was dealing with depression and suicidal thoughts. I watched my youngest daughter isolate herself from everyone and I was trying to encourage her, but behind closed doors I was experiencing depression also. God was trying to birth something out of me. I often asked God, "What are you trying to get out of me? What test are you giving me that I keep failing?" I realized I was always over analyzing things trying to make sense of everything. I had many doors open and was allowing people to bring their storms into my life, and God had to teach me how to pray and release their burdens. Finally, I was walking into the year of 2020 focused on God healing, fulfilling and making me whole.

2020 was the year of perfect vision, momentum and acceleration, the year to stay consistent and accomplish goals. I heard all around the world on social media about 2020 being the year of acceleration. Even in my personal life God was speaking to me about what building he was placing in my hands to build. As soon as 2020 came in, within three months the world was shaken because some famous people, who made a major impact in the lives of people, lost their lives. For a while, the world was hurting because of this tragedy. Many people were surprised by how the new year started out. However, everyone was still talking about slaying goals, going back to school, starting businesses and just trying to stay optimistic about the powerful prophetic word that was given. Shortly after there was an outbreak of Covid-19, the Corona Virus that affected China. People were getting sick and dying, but it got real once it reached the United States. There were so many speculations that only certain races could get affected with the virus, and that there weren't any African Americans catching the virus. That was a myth, because shortly after so many people all over the world were affected. This caused a state of emergency and we were ordered to be quarantined. All over the world, people's faith was tested. This pandemic caused a lot of people to lose their jobs and business owners were closing their businesses. People didn't know where their next meal was going to come from. Depending on God was more important now because our nation was in a crisis. So, the government had to pass a bill of 2 trillion dollars so people could pay their bills and also to put back into the economy. The bill gave money to workers, parents and children. The relief funds helped, but it wasn't enough money. Many companies weren't even able to stay afloat because there weren't many people spending money in order to keep the economy going. You can say that the money was not available to spend. I felt like the whole world was shaken, even believers.

As a child I was taught that fear was not of God. I saw the supernatural right in front of my face. But, during the pandemic, I had to ask God "What's going on Lord?" The spirit of fear was creeping up on me. I had a quick reality check and I realized that no matter what I was going through, that God was still in control. This virus killed millions of people and every day I prayed for the nation, including every household. I prayed for the mental health of the people because the people hadn't seen a virus that shook the nation up.

In the midst of the pandemic, God's hands were still moving. People were birthing businesses, books, platforms, buying homes, and even getting a closer relationship with God. As an entrepreneur, God was allowing people that I did not know to support my business. I made more money in a famine and pandemic than I had ever made since I started my business. I was being blessed, and I also loved seeing others get blessed, not only with their spiritual walk but in their everyday lives.

Although the pandemic was rough, I was able to go through with God. Even in the midst of this chaotic situation I was thriving and watching others around me soar. In the bible, Proverbs 13:22 says that the wealth of the wicked is stored up for the righteous. God's word is all facts. Some relationships ended and some marriages were starting and blooming. God was providing for his children and obedience to God's words was going to help us survive during this time.

CHAPTER 23

People Hurt

I WAS BROUGHT UP IN CHURCH IN THE PENTECOSTAL, HOLINESS AND fire baptized movement. Later on, my grandma started a non-denominational ministry where her ministry was Holy Spirit led. I joined my grandma's ministry and I was very active. She was teaching, equipping, and grooming me as a young woman in God. My grandma was a dynamic pastor that preached the true gospel and taught and encouraged me how to walk upright in God. Like every ministry, our church had problems, but it was quickly handled and the focus and agenda were doing God's will.

Because of past emotional and mental abuse from family, I decided to part ways, and later I joined another ministry. I was not a religious person, but I came from the religious era and I was a stickler on some things. Even as a child, I was big on love because of the teaching and demonstration I had seen. So, I left my grandma's church and embarked on a new journey and relied on God for myself. I wanted to break free from some of the family culture and follow Christ. I was invited to a new ministry by my cousin and shortly after I joined.

Because of my background and what I was taught, it was hard to adapt to the new church culture. When I was at my old ministry, I felt like I was growing, but at this new ministry, I felt like I was stuck and being held back. I was no longer that bold in the Lord young lady that I once was. My mouth was muzzled. I felt like I was in bondage and hindered from doing what God was calling me to do. I would get crazy looks because I was full of the Holy Spirit and some people had a problem with the Holy

Spirit, even though it is in the bible. Also, as a young married woman with three children, when I came into the ministry I was looked down on as if I wasn't good enough because of status or class.

When I was a babe in Christ, I realized that I was a work in progress. I still needed grace and mercy, and I was grateful that grace abounded in my shortcomings. Even though I felt like I was at a place of recovery from childhood trauma, I was a broken woman who trusted that one day I would be fulfilled in God. No amount of pain that I experienced in my past would deter me from my destiny. I continued to go to church because I knew that the church was the place for love, healing, truth, correction, deliverance and much more.

When I use the phrase "church hurt", I mean "people hurt" because I am the church. After leaving the church I grew up in, I experienced enormous abuse from leaders that I trusted as spiritual parents. The lack of equipping leaders and lack of accountability caused pain that affected myself and my children. There were other members who were mishandled as well. However, I recall some members telling me that the reason why they continued to come to church anyway was because of the way my own family loved on them. Unfortunately, the church lacked God's love and compassion. I know how it feels to be betrayed, overlooked, and rejected. I remember feeling like the church had become a business, and the lost was no longer getting delivered. It was the same familiarity and I was ready to see the full manifestation of God. Man's agenda had gotten in the way of God's intent for the church.

There was a leader who was a major hindrance in the church. Although she led multiple functions in the ministry, she was having issues with people in the church.. I saw the enemy in her working against me. She was controlling and inserted her way of doing things in God's house. There was no unity, and the love was different than what I was used to. I was raised in an era in the church where the mothers loved on you as soon as you walked in the church and encouraged you in your walk with God.

In this church, I felt like my family was the target with labels being placed on my children and myself from church members. One day after dealing with these ongoing issues, I was called into a church meeting, and I blew up. It was bad! I mean the conversation got heated. Because of the continued abuse and built-up frustrations, I reacted ungodly and became angry and said some things that I could not take back. I reverted back to the culture in which I grew up—that fighting nature. Shortly after I went off, I was convicted instantly, and I felt ashamed. It did not take long for God to chastise me because of my own actions. I felt so bad because I felt like I disappointed God and let down people that looked up to me. I realized later that the situation was simply because some women envied my life.

No one prayed before the meeting to even set an atmosphere of love. The deaconess that was in charge of the meeting did not have the right heart posture and because of the way she came at me, I felt attacked and I reacted. I was frustrated because she didn't address me in love. In reality, she was also a problem in the ministry. On numerous occasions she would offend other people, but her behavior was always excused. I was so hurt because when I responded without self-control, no one showed me understanding.

After the meeting I was treated badly. No one would stand with me, not even my husband who was also a member of the church. I was treated differently. I was shunned by leaders on several occasions. Even after I apologized, there was no grace. It took me to meet someone special to restore me back to health.

God has people everywhere. One night while working third shift at my second job, I was sitting next to a woman of God. We began to talk and I found out she was an ordained minister. On my way to the car, she started speaking into my life, confirming some things that I was going through. She told me to tell my husband to stand with me.

I wore a mask every day I came to church, not a mask for people but because I was a wounded spirit and I was hiding. Meanwhile my children saw more than necessary. One lesson I am grateful that my mom taught me was to stick together as a family. I definitely instilled the same information in my children. I realized that I allowed my loyalty to people to get in the way of my responsibility to God. I had to lean on God. I really wanted leaders that helped nurture and bring the gifts out of all the members, not just their favorites. So, I was offended at the time and bitter because of the things that I was witnessing in my ministry. My spirit was vexed by the control, manipulation, and usury that was going on. However, I continued to stay faithful to that ministry, even though the Lord was telling me that my season was up.

I stayed at that church until I realized that my oldest Dontae was starting to despise church and lose respect for people he thought so highly of. He was becoming bitter, not only because his mother was getting treated wrong, but because of the comments that were made about him. For example, he was told that his tattoos on his arms were a big problem, even though he was a good black young male without a record.

After enduring abuse from the wrong ministry, I was told to leave. I had a hard time adjusting to the new age church because I had been taught to always have a heart for people. Church wasn't the same at all. The new word doctrine did not convey the Holy Spirit, which is the best teacher. What I read in the word of God was not displayed in the church. There was confusion from the word of God. The church was full of cliques, without a godly love language. There were hurt people and some leaders weren't equipped to deal with the people that were in a hurt stage. So, my heart was heavy and I continued to pray for the body of Christ asking God to intervene. There were some doctrines that I put on the shelf until God gave me the illumination. Sometimes God would tell me to hold on to what was already planted on the inside.

God entrusts shepherds with his sheep, but we at one point felt like the black sheep of the ministry. I even remember the different curses spoken against my children by leaders. I prayed for God to burn those curses up immediately.

As I reflect on my experiences, I wish that I had not operated out of emotion and handled things the way the bible teaches us how to deal with issues and offenses. However, one thing I learned in life is how to persevere. I did a lot of praying and learned how to forgive others as well as myself. I was trying to protect my reputation, but God changed my perspective about the situation. God said, "Allow me to rebuild your character. When you are dealing with so much warfare it's important for you to do what the bible instructs you to do." The bible teaches us how to fight and how specific scriptures can be applied to our lives. Before, I allowed myself to fight a spiritual fight naturally. So, I reacted out of anger because I was tired of feeling like the bad sheep and like our family wasn't good enough. But, I realized that sometimes I have to be okay with not getting an apology.

With the way I was raised and by spending time with God, I learned how to make my wrongs right. I went to several people and apologized for any wrong or offense I may have said and done against them.

Over the years, I have seen so many Christians walk in unforgiveness because God would show me their hearts. However, the bible clearly teaches us to forgive, and if there is any offense done, we are to go to them to make it right. This reality at one point of my life scorned me. I really felt like I did not want to be a Christian, if this is what it all entailed. I was a spiritual mess. I did not want to serve in the house of God anymore. I died in a ministry and did not realize I was dying. I did not have the zeal that I used to have for the Lord. The spirit of jealousy was rising up in people that were supposed to cover me but instead hindered my growth. I started believing that I was not a necessary part of the body of Christ. I allowed myself to endure spiritual abuse for about 9 years and the shepherds that were called to shepherd me mishandled me.

I was so caught up in being loyal to people that it caused me to disobey God. I was called to evangelize and spread the gospel of Jesus Christ, and I wasn't walking in my calling. I was spiritually sick, and I wasn't doing God's will. I was stuck in hurt, pain, and depression and I couldn't seem to get out of the rut that I was in. I did not want to have anything to do with the church or God's people. There were some days that I would weep all through the night laying in my bed, even some mornings. Betrayal from people you love hurts, especially when you have a heart for people.

I started questioning God, "Who am I, what is my purpose, and why is life so hard?" I remember believing the negative things that were spoken over my life. The spirit of shame was all over me. I started to feel unworthy of walking in my calling.

I was always trying to prove my truth, until the day God told me to stop. Although I was lied on, I realized people sometimes want to believe the worst about you.

One day, I visited a church and a lady prophesied to me, "People love telling lies and speaking ill against your name, but God is going to defend you. "I realized at this point that my character alone was going to speak for me. When you have outgrown a place it's time to move on. Don't get so caught up on loyalty to people instead of obeying God. Doing what God told me to do disappointed some people, but I was okay with that because I realized I spent so many years pleasing people.

After all the rejection and being shunned, I walked away from toxic relationships, and I started dispatching myself from people and places that were not helping me reach my next level in God. I realized that some relationships are meant to only be forgiven, not restored, because God knows what's in the heart of men. The moral of the story is that rejection was a blessing because it was protecting me from what was not meant for me.

I remember being at home praying and seeking God's face about the next move. For six months we only had church at home. I was a little hesitant to join a new ministry because of the fear of rumors and of my past church experiences. After spending time with God and praying, my husband and I visited a church that my husband's cousin was attending. We visited preferably three times and the Lord told my husband and me that this was the place that we needed to be planted. There was an authentic worship and love of God in the atmosphere which drew me. The sermon that the pastor preached that transformed my life was "Love Thy Neighbor as Thyself". I will never forget this message because he reiterated the message about ten times until it resonated in my spirit. From that day, I made the decision to forgive and move forward, even if people did not know my side of the story. I knew it was time to leave my old ministry in the past and move forward.

I had asked God to, not only allow me to grow in the word, but I wanted a ministry where my family could be active and love being a part of different ministries in the church. God did just that in this new ministry. My middle daughter was an usher and my youngest daughter praise danced and mimed. God knew exactly what we needed. I was doing what I love! I was teaching the youth the word of God! I truly enjoy teaching biblical truths and demonstrating the love of Christ.

I was grateful to experience a ministry where I was able to learn and serve. I was a teacher teaching the teens and it was rewarding. I am grateful that I had leaders that truly loved on me and helped and equipped me for the work of the Lord.

CHAPTER 24

My Girl Boss Experience

I WAS FULL OF GIFTS AND TALENTS AND WAS PASSIONATE ABOUT BUSINESS, but I self-sabotaged myself for many years. One day, I decided to join a women's business group that was full of CEOs and corporate women, and I was so excited to finally be around incubators and accelerators. Being around women of their caliber helped influence me to step my game up. I came from humble beginnings and had been selling products for as long as I could remember. I started selling out of my trunk and making connections by word of mouth.

2018 was the year that I was pondering about getting these business goals off the ground. I was a little discouraged because I had just gotten married, and opening a store wasn't really in the budget. I knew this was the year that God said it was time to jump, step out on faith and walk in my purpose. I was so overwhelmed, and during pillow talk with my husband, he told me, "Baby, don't get discouraged. Everything is going to work out. Why don't you start online until we are able to buy a storefront?" That made so much sense! My husband supported me during the building process. He allowed me to pocket some of my money to save for the business until I reached 4,000.00 dollars for my business startup. I was so glad I was not allowing another year to go by without walking in my purpose. I realized that researching and starting a business was very time consuming and sometimes not having the resources could hinder my business from excelling. As a business owner, I was able to see my areas of weakness and strength. One of my strengths was my interaction with people. I loved interacting with my customers, picking out nice clothes and making them feel beautiful. Due to trial and error, I realized that the marketing part of my business sucked. Actually, a lot of people did not know that I even had an online boutique.

After a year, my business was really picking up, and I started getting more attention. I realized that money is only a portion of starting a business. If you want your business to be successful, then your marketing must be everything. I started doing research all through the night to educate myself on apps and resources that would make my business stand out. Oftentimes many business owners fail to have a CTA known as a call to action, which is content such as promotions and discounts that allow audiences to jump on deals.

It takes a strong team to help push a business to the next level, but I made the mistake of trying to run a business on my own and became, once again, overwhelmed. So, a relative told me that God laid it on her heart to help push my business to the next level. She helped me with more of the marketing side of my business. My sister wore and modeled my clothes and showed up at pop-up shops to assist me in whatever I needed help with. My mom was my biggest supporter and was big on word of mouth. My whole team was my immediate family helping with everything from inventory to organizing clothes.

As I was going into year 2 of my business, God placed it on my heart to reinvent my business. So, I started all over by adding to my business plan. To take my business to the next level, I connected with a good friend who helped me with my LLCs and EIN, and later on I created a dope website. I also created business boards and spoke things in the atmosphere, making goals that had nothing to do with my pocketbook, but faith. I realized at this point that my business was in God's hands. God had given me the vision and he would give me provision for my business. At times when I saw people soaring in their businesses, I would take my eyes off of how God was orchestrating and building my business. I had to shift my focus and continue to learn and grow in my business.

I went back to the drawing board with my business. In the beginning of my process, I felt stuck because I did not know at the time who I could connect with in order to bring my business to life. I remember speaking to one of my relatives over the phone about business goals. Not only did we talk about what I wanted to accomplish but, I also encouraged her to pursue her dreams. One day she called me and told me that she had a dream about my business becoming big and it became overwhelming. She said, "God told me to assist you with your business goals."

I thought it was a great decision to bring my cousin on board to assist me with my business due to the fact we both have a strong passion for entrepreneurship. I am a visionary who is knowledgeable about business, and my cousin was knowledgeable about graphic and marketing aspects of business. She assisted me with logos and flyers and found me two vendors during the time of my building process.

Shortly after, my cousin started her hair and beauty business and she had an amazing launch. I was so excited for her that I lent her a business loan to help bring everything together. I was a major asset to her business and I assisted and supported her business. I also assisted her with financial support for housing. However, what was done with pure intent would later be met with betrayal. Later on, I found out through connections with friends and family that my cousin was taking credit for my business. I was so hurt because I extended my support to her as a mentor, encourager, and prayer partner. So, I completely disconnected myself from her because her intentions weren't pure.

I began to identify the problem in my business, and realized that I needed to hire a new team and delegate. I began to train my teenage daughters. Also, one day God told me to call my sister. It was a smooth transition because the new team aligned with my business vision. I continued to focus on my business and kept building.

My daughters and the others on my team became stronger because these were the people who were supposed to be a part of my team. I was so happy because God sent me people that were a blessing to my team with nothing to gain. I was also excited about what the year would bring in. I received a powerful prophetic word about what God was going to do with my business. During a regular conversation with my best friend, God began to use her in a mighty way. "The Lord is going to give everything you need for your business to be successful. Don't worry about anything. God is going to do it. Though they slay you, trust God. Don't worry about anything. God is fighting for you." I received that word that the Lord spoke through her and remained prayerful and focused on God's word knowing that God would finish what he started in me. Instead of trying to prove myself to people, I realized that God had the power to do whatever he was going to do in my business. I learned how to write down the prophetic words that God spoke into my life and watched them come to pass. I was told many years prior to starting my business that it was going to be prosperous. So, I did not need another word. I just needed to trust the word that God had already given me.

While on an entrepreneurial journey, I have learned that having a business will cause you to see your strengths and weaknesses. I learned that failure is a part of success, but I should not allow failure to be the reason to give up what God gave me to start and build.

CHAPTER 25

God Changing My Perspective Concerning Betrayal And Disappointments

A s I GOT OLDER, I JUST LOOKED AT LIFE DIFFERENTLY. YES, I FELT betrayed and disappointed about some of my experiences that I had with individuals that I trusted, whether it was family, relationships, or friendships. I was so disappointed to find out that some people, that I actually thought I could build with, had the wrong motives. Ever since I was a teenage girl, I couldn't trust people because of past experiences of jealousy. I sometimes would stay in bad company, though, just so I did not feel alone. I just wanted to feel like I was a part of something.

The older I got the more I realized that I had to love me more than that. Even if the people who were in my life didn't appreciate or value me, I had to be the first partaker of self-love and self-care. I continued to pray that God would send me authentic people who were not connected to me because of their need for me.

The majority of my betrayal experiences came from family members. In my teenage years is when I first experienced betrayal. For example, I met a guy who I really liked, and I hooked my cousin up with his cousin, so we could go out on a double date. After my boyfriend's cousin and my cousin connected and talked over the phone, I received a call from my boyfriend and his cousin. They asked me, "Are you sure that those ladies are your cousins?"

I said, "Yes, why do you ask?"

"Because they were talking about you badly behind your back."

He also gave names, and I knew there was some truth to what I was told. I got so upset and my mother told me, "Do things solo. No one needs to know your business. Be more private about things."

There was so much competition in my family with the adults and the children. Family members were sleeping with each other's boyfriends, and backbiting. Jealousy and animosity were normal in my family. But, not everyone in the family was like that. I was taught to respect the female code and to be lady-like. This confusion affected me badly. I became cautious and suspicious of people. As I grew up, I started to separate myself from my family and created my own family. Oftentimes I got backlash, but I realized that blood alone doesn't make you family. It's how you value each other.

One of the hardest betrayals that shifted my mindset and gave me a different view of making decisions and seeking God for everything was when I was betrayed by a family member that I thought had my best interest at heart and really supported my vision. I would help family members who had intent to betray and sabotage my life, but God would always turn it around for my good. Jealousy will have you mishandle people who were sent to bless you. I realized forgiveness was my job as a believer, but some people I had to detach myself from and move on. I remember when my grandma dropped gems on me. She said, "The same enemy that was in that person when they did what they did before is the same enemy that is in them until deliverance happens."

I was angry and shocked because of the rumors spreading about me and my immediate family, so I began to remove the people out of my life that did not mean me any good. Even though I cut some people off I had to release them out of my spirit. I had to remind myself of who I was and to not hold people hostage because of being crossed by them and talked about. I realized that I had to do a heart check and make sure that I wasn't harboring anger, strife, and unforgiveness in my heart. Now it was time for me to let go and move forward and allow God to deal with them. The bible says the heart is deceitful and I wasn't going to block my blessings by holding on to the past. Forgiveness is hard, but it is necessary. I had to learn how to distance myself from people that did not mean me any good and not hold them hostage in my heart, but forgive as my father forgives.

Built up jealousy and hatred were passed down from our parents and it put a wedge between family members. It was like history repeating itself, but it stopped with me. My children were disappointed with what they heard and were truly concerned, but I had to continue to teach them what it is to have a healthy functioning family. At this point is where I learned what God was trying to show me concerning the company that I kept. Because God had matured me, this betrayal did not break me nor shake me. God exposed who was in my life and before he elevated me the right ones had to be in my life. Every day I began to walk proud with my head held high because I knew man did not give me this joy and no number of rumors could take it away.

This journey called life has taught me so many lessons. Oftentimes, I felt that God was punishing me because I dealt with so much warfare from childhood to adulthood. However, God was positioning me to do his will. Isaiah 66:9 ERV "*in the same way I will not cause pain without allowing something new to be born, says your God.*" I realized God had a divine purpose for my life, and even my enemies couldn't stop God's plans for my life. I understood that the pain I endured wasn't in vain. I learned that I had to consult God about everything. Even in my eagerness God was number 1 concerning all my decisions. God also told me to forgive and let go of any offense. Moving forward I had to set boundaries and guard my heart. I no longer felt guilty, or was being manipulated to do things without God's approval. My life became simpler because I understood my place and that it was okay to allow God to be everything for people. I did not have to feel like everyone was my assignment, and I could release their heavy burdens.

CHAPTER 26

Married Life

MARRIAGE IS HARD WORK AND GOD HAS TO BE IN THE CENTER OF A marriage. As a woman, I had to continue to pray and intercede on behalf of my marriage in the midst of grief, pain, pandemic, and loss. As a godly wife, I wore many hats. I was losing family members back-to- back, and my heart was in pain. Even with the many struggles that my husband and I were dealing with, God taught me how to love beyond flaws because love holds no account of wrong. Some women admired what they felt my lifestyle was. They had no clue that I was just a working wife, mother, and most importantly a child of God. Some people don't understand the need to rush into marriage until the challenges and the opposition comes. I wanted my marriage to exemplify a godly image because marriage is honorable before the Lord. I knew my desire and how marriage is ministry. There is power in unity and a marriage that honors God.

There were times where being a wife was so overwhelming that I wanted to walk away. I understand now so vividly that your moral backgrounds and how you both imagine marriage to be are so vitally important when it comes to marriage. What I envisioned marriage to be was togetherness, oneness, having a prayer partner, and a man that covered me as his wife. I definitely imagined a man that was the head of the family and that heard from God to lead his family. However, I wasn't seeing this demonstration in the household, though I saw a great servant outside the home. This situation provoked me to pray and stay in God's word. I was disappointed, but most importantly I prayed more. The more I prayed the more I saw God's hand in the midst of our marriage.

My husband and I have such a large family which oftentimes wasn't easy but, God blessed us both with the capacity to love, encourage, and pour into our children and lead by example. I had to be a wife with dignity, restraint, and a sober mind. I continued to love even in the midst of our marital struggles because God is love and love covers a multitude of sins.

Some of my single friends sometimes had false assumptions of what they thought my marriage was. I began to remind them that marriage is hard work. When you see peace, love, grace, and understanding, just know God was working behind the scenes.

God showed me that I needed to surround myself with more married people to gain strength and to see what Godly marriages look like. I was able to receive wisdom from my married friends that helped us navigate through some marital rough patches. I continued to look up to God for healing and restoration in our marriage. God has the power to fix what is broken.

CHAPTER 27

Taking Back My Power

NEGATIVE WORDS HAVE THE POWER TO CRIPPLE YOU. WORDS ARE SO powerful and have the potential to shape your reality, whether they are words of life or death. For many years I allowed others to project their perception of what they felt I was, and oftentimes I believed them. I watched words kill dreams and the spirit of people prematurely.

I had to learn how to control my emotions concerning the things that were sent to destroy my peace. I struggled in this area. I was defensive which stemmed from my past childhood experiences. As a child, I dealt with slanderous words spoken against me. So, I allowed my emotions to dictate my decisions for years and responded to things without allowing God to lead me.

Everyone has their own individual struggles, but mine was overcoming the labels and the lies put on me by others. I cared too much about how people felt about me, which led me to feel insecure and insignificant about my worth. There were rumors about me that weren't true. Of course, no one is perfect and there were some things that I had done in life that I wasn't proud of. But I understand now why I did certain things and responded the way I responded. The culture I was raised in helped shape my reality.

My biggest issue that I battled with growing up was I was a people pleaser. Even as a five-year-old girl, I wanted to fit in. I remember going to a catholic school and being the new girl in the classroom. I was so glad to have friends even if they weren't really nice to me. I was connected to little mean girls even in kindergarten. One of the little girls tried to fight me in the bathroom. She began to tease me and started laughing. I was so hurt because I knew at that point, we were no longer friends. I remember the feeling I felt of embarrassment and shame because I knew they weren't really nice friends. I also knew that they were going to walk out of my life because I was already used to being abandoned.

I remember feeling that if no one else loved me, I should always have love from my extended family, not just my immediate family. Oftentimes I would go around family members where there were constant feuds and competition. I knew that a lot of the family drama came from our parents who had unresolved jealousy issues with each other. However, I felt as an adult that all the drama we had as children was in the past. So, one day I went out of town with my grown cousins to Columbus, Ohio, where I could enjoy and have a ball with my family. We laughed, grilled out and had a whole feast at my auntie's house. Later that night, we went to a bar and grill and shot pool. I mean we had a ball! On our way back to the city— we were not even on the highway for an hour— I started experiencing the same toxic behaviors that I remembered dealing with as a child. On the highway, my mom received a phone call about unnecessary petty conversations concerning me. I was told that I was copying off a particular cousin because I had purchased a newer model Chevy Impala. God had opened up the door for me to have my car, so I felt no need to respond to the ignorant conversation. I was also told from this particular aunt how this cousin despised me. In the car I said, "This is the same ole dysfunctional family stuff and it is time for me to separate myself again." As a grown woman now, I didn't have to allow myself to be around family to be loved and accepted.

After realizing that I had no desire to stay connected to toxic relationships, no matter who they were, family, friends, etc., and that I no longer wanted to be a people pleaser, God showed me that I could protect my peace, forgive and move on.

As a woman who knows who I am in God, people putting false labels on me does not cancel out who God says I am. Misunderstandings, people's suspicions and other false narratives about me no longer shake me. Oftentimes God has already revealed to me how some people feel concerning me, so I do not have to worry about it. I've learned how to give people over to God without slandering their names. There are so many levels to growing that I didn't even understand my own ignorance. I was defensive and offended all the time. But God would close my mouth and I couldn't speak even against my enemies. God told me that he would vindicate me. This was very hard for me because I grew up in a culture where harsh talking was the norm and I was exposed to it at a very early age. So, when I became saved it was hard to make that transition. Oftentimes, I was told I was a peacemaker, but when I was dealing with conflict my voice would elevate. I realized that I wasn't any different from my enemies because I fought my battles with a carnal mind. But now, I no longer defend my name and reputation. I allow God to uphold me and I show godly love even from a distance.

Learning to let go and accept things I cannot change is a valuable lesson I learned in life. Growing up, I felt like I did something wrong because my father would not really accept me as his daughter and build a father and daughter relationship with me. Oftentimes I felt like he was a stranger and we lived in the same city. I was tired of being the girl that had daddy issues. I realized it was not my job to be the parent, but, at the time, to be the little girl whose father was supposed to initiate the relationship building process. For many years we would connect and talk on the phone for a while, but he then would go missing again.

One day my daughter's great auntie on their dad's side passed away. When I walked into the funeral there was my dad showing support and embracing the family for their loss. I remember feeling angry because I couldn't even count on him to support me. I couldn't even recall this man telling me that he loved me, and that alone broke my heart. Oftentimes, even as an adult, I continued to blame my mother for my dad not being in my life. In 2020 I tried to reach out to my father once again and he changed his number on me. I felt like that little girl again longing for her father. I knew that at this point I needed to move forward. After my attempt to reach out to him wasn't successful, that night I prayed for him and his family and asked God to bless him. I knew I had matured and grown when I began praying for my father. My prayer was that before he leaves this earth that he would reach out to me and understand that I love him no matter what he did to me. I also prayed that he would forgive himself and the others that hurt him. One thing I learned from my father is that he felt so unloved as a young boy growing up. He felt like he was not good enough and was treated unfairly like his other siblings. I often wondered why he afflicted hurt on his child, if he knew what it was like to be hurt. I remember asking my father, "Why can't you forgive people that hurt you so you can be free?"

I had to unlearn some things and behaviors that I had adapted to. I had to learn not to allow conflict to override the things that needed immediate attention at that moment. Not every criticism and correction are meant to destroy me, but some things are meant to help me grow and develop into who God called me to be.

CHAPTER 28

On A Journey Of Healing

H EALING IS ESSENTIAL. IT ALLOWS A DEEPER LEVEL OF HEALTHY growth and clarity of one's purpose, while having the capacity of love, forgiveness, and fulfillment in God. Healing allows you to extend grace to those that did the offense, understanding that God also gives us grace for our offenses. I am no longer walking in the form of healing, but God is totally healing me.

God is removing every unfruitful residue from my heart. God is dealing with those hidden issues of my heart and healing those unhealthy wounds. While on this healing journey I have learned to fully love because my love is not determined by how anyone feels about me. I have also learned to love people where they are, not burdening myself with who reciprocates that love or not.

While on a healing journey I have learned that everyone's healing is different and should not ever be compared. The healing process looks different on each individual. Two people can experience the same trauma and respond or behave differently. Oftentimes it's based on our perspective concerning the trauma and turmoil we experienced in life. Many times, I heard people say, "Oh, I've been through rejection, but I am good. I am healed from it." Rejection for me was deeply rooted in me, and only God had the power to deliver me. At one point of my life, I wondered why rejection was such a thorn for me, but I realized that both of my parents were rejected. I also realized that we cannot downplay or ignore our past experiences. Instead, we need to heal from them.

On my journey of healing, I realized that all that I had endured from childhood, adolescence, and even adulthood wasn't in vain. I no longer despised the things that cultivated me. I realized that I did not ask for the trauma, pain, and feelings of feeling misplaced in life, but it was definitely my responsibility to heal from it.

I repetitiously rehashed those past wounds for years. I was reliving those painful memories by not healing from them. It's not that what I experienced in my past didn't happen, but it no longer existed because it was in my past. I was just dealing with the after effects from the past. One day I was so grateful that I have the Holy Spirit. I was driving in the car taking my mind down memory lane, just bringing up the old hurt, and past experiences, and God checked me. I heard God's voice very clearly, "STOP REHEARSING YOUR PAST HURT!" I knew it was time to move forward in healing. Just that quick God reminded me how he kept me in the midst of my trials.

I realized as an unhealed woman that my children gleaned from my depression, isolation, and limited beliefs. My children deserved a healed version of their mother. Once I identified my children as a mirror of their mother, I had to watch my reflection. I was committed to change so that healing would show up in every aspect of my life.

I had to be vulnerable with God by not putting walls up and allowing God to completely heal me in my broken areas. Oftentimes I was not considered a genuine person because I would only allow people to get so close to me. Because of betrayal I wasn't exposing my true self, only the mask version of myself. I could only let my hair down around people that I could trust and be vulnerable around them.

Self-reflection is a powerful tool when it comes to healing because, as I got older, so did the trauma. Some of my behavior in life was because of the cultural things that I was exposed to early on. I watched some of my family members endure great pain and tragedy in life, and some things they didn't recover from.

I was allowed to identify my faults and truths and make my corrections. I understood that even as a grown woman I was in pain. God had given me the gift to see people for who they were, so I wasn't always doing what the bible says about loving my enemies. Oftentimes I would have limited interactions with them because I knew the truth about who they were. My heart was harboring unhealthy fruits. I prayed daily for God to search my heart. Even in the midst of my heart needing surgery, I saw God begin to clean and mature me. Self-reflection also allowed me to search deep within myself and understand why I tolerated unhealthy connections for seasons after seasons in my life. I was able to see things so clearly, understanding that the enemy was after my oil and trying to keep me exhausted, frustrated, and too depressed to serve God. As much as I felt like I was not necessary in the kingdom, God showed me otherwise. I began to realize that I was a threat to the enemy's kingdom. That is why the enemy wanted to annihilate me. I am a weeping intercessor and daughter of the most high God. Despite how long I was in the dark about who I was, knowing my identity in Christ set my life on fire.

What God says about you will always hold weight over what man says about you. I remember feeling so free from shame, guilt, and humiliation. I learned to forgive myself when I fell short or in error and continued to live a narrow road to salvation. I learned to give myself grace and continued to grow in God. I am not healed completely, but I am in the process of healing and I realize that healing is my portion no matter what. Some things God healed me from in just three days, and some things had to happen in a process, but I know that I serve a God that loves me for me and has the power to restore me. I choose to be free in God and not allow anyone to control, manipulate, and tell me who I am not in God. I have access to Jesus for myself and I am glad that he has never left nor forsaken me. I know now that God has called me to encourage people, to show the love of Christ through my actions and to pray for the nation, even my enemies. I really love the fact that God gave me a women's ministry to encourage and influence women to identify their purpose, spiritually and naturally, and walk into it. That's so important. Many women are broken and need healing in order to be their best as a woman, wife, leader, friend, and parent. It is okay to seek extra help. In other words, I can pray and see a counselor in order to be mentally healthy.

I am proud of my women's group that God gave to me. I am growing in areas that I felt I was doomed in. I didn't ever think that I could be mentally healthy, but depression doesn't have dominion over me anymore. God has given me power to speak to my mountain and tell it to move. I am no longer bound to people's perceptions of me. I have been forgiven. God has delivered me from the approval of men. Knowing who I am in God is far more important. Sometimes we expect people to jump on board with what God has called you to do, but what God has for you is for you. I had to learn to remove all negative labels and remain true to myself.

I learned how to be quiet, and not be so quick to get angry when dealing with opposition. Everything about me started to shift because my perceptions about who I am in God shifted. My language to God has changed the way I pray and how I come before his presence. The bible tells us that when we pray, we are to ask in the name of Jesus. If God doesn't answer, then we asked with the wrong motives. I had to check my motives about everything that I spoke out of my mouth. I realized I have power in my tongue to speak life or death. I began to speak, "I am already healed," and I believed that God had already done it.

Part of my healing was being okay with not being liked by everyone and understanding that Jesus was rejected yet continued to go about his father's business. I learned how to live without telling my side of the story because God knows and sees all. I can recall praying on the phone with one of my prophet friends and God using her in a mighty way. She gave me a powerful word directly from God. "Though they slay you, trust God. Though they persecute you, God said keep trusting him. No matter what, he will take your business to the next level. Don't worry about anything. Stop explaining yourself to people. God sees all." I was dealing with things concerning my business and people coming up against me, yet again God told me to keep my mouth shut and I did. I obeyed God because I realized God would vindicate me. That word was definitely a confirmation because God told me, "Let them misunderstand you. I will hold up a standard." Sometimes it's important to stop trying to defend your reputation to people who only want to see the worst in you.

Be okay with people not understanding where you are in your healing process. At the time while I was going through those old wounds, some people thought I was a victim. Not knowing that pain was embedded so deeply in me, I despised the pain I was enduring because it affected everything about me. I realized as a child that I did not ask for trauma, pain, or abuse, but healing was my responsibility.

I could no longer run away from what I was experiencing, but healing was a choice. One time God showed me the chatter that was said about me concerning my healing. God did not allow me to respond, but instead to focus on my healing and change my mindset. I knew that whatever I experienced growing up as a child was not going to disappear, but it no longer had power over me. During my journey of healing God gave me three categories for my healing. Simple words but, with great meaning. Healthy habits, setting boundaries, and self-love.

Between 2019-2020 I felt like my emotions were jacked up and I wasn't guarding my heart and protecting my treasure. However, now I was walking in healing. It felt so good not to care about the spectators and what man had to say about me. I knew my validation came from God. I was at a place with God that it did not matter who was against me, or who wasn't in agreement with the assignment that God called me to.

One day God downloaded strategies in me to help me on my healing journey. For many years I prayed for healing and wholeness in God. I knew it was time to unpack all of the painful baggage and allow my healing to take place. He gave me healthy habits, setting boundaries, self-love, and to go deeper. One day as my mother was in consecration, I was dealing with warfare at my job. My mother called and she began to pray for me. The powerful word that came out of her mouth was, "Oftentimes we struggle with trauma, loss, and opposition, but we cannot allow everyone access to us." At that moment this powerful conversation hit me in a powerful way. It shifted my whole intellect. I realized that the rejected little girl in me was giving so much of myself to people and places where I wasn't valued.

Setting Boundaries

Setting boundaries is so important that it should be a priority. It's extremely important to self- examine yourself. For many years I was a ticking time bomb. I was always angry. I did not know how to filter my emotions. I would instantly go into defense mode when I felt like I was getting attacked. I remember talking to God. "Lord, I believe I have a little anger management issue." I would always talk about my children having issues, but I had to identify my own issues I was dealing with. I was exposed knowing that I wasn't perfect. I also learned that I didn't guard my heart and eye and ear gates.

I had to learn to set boundaries for myself as well as my children. I realized the youth are at the mercy of society and their parents. The youth look up to their parents and those who care for them to protect them. My mother protected me from many unhealthy relationships, but she did not completely remove me from the abuse and cursed words that I experienced growing up. The older I got, the more I started setting boundaries. When I was 14 years old, one of my aunties would always call me a whore even though I was a virgin. At the age of 18, I had my first apartment, and I started standing up for myself and demanding respect. As I got older, I felt sorry for my auntie for normalizing curse words. She had three daughters that did not know how to lift each other up and edify one another. So, I realized that it was okay to love people from a distance.

Access Denied

I had to learn there are some doors that need to be shut completely, not giving everyone access to my life. I had to know when to walk away from some people, even in the church. God continued to reveal the hearts of people I thought were really for me and taught me how to walk away. Sometimes it's a painful reality especially when you love God's people, but not everyone has God's spirit.

I had to also set boundaries concerning who I allowed to have access to me and when they had access to me. Growing up, I was following in my grandma's footsteps. She was a blesser. She went above and beyond for people, and that was me. I was the oldest sibling and I was a caregiver for everyone without boundaries. People took advantage of my giving and generosity. Family oftentimes, used to be dependent on me. I was supportive of family and friends until it seemed like a burden instead. Later on, after marriage and having three children, I had to focus on my household. A friend began to point out how I looked so tired and sluggish. As a Christian woman she began to tell me, "You cannot be everything to everyone all the time. You have to say no sometimes." She asked me, "How does being so busy help your household?" I thought that she made a valid point. This conversation freed my mindset. I began to say no sometimes and not feel guilty for saying it.

Creating Healthy Habits

Creating healthy habits was a strategy that really shifted my mindset and helped me gain control of my life. One night as I laid in the bed, my mind was overloaded with so much because I have always been a major thinker. Some thoughts made me very frustrated and I became overwhelmed. I was focused on life and the different things that were going on. Being a mother to my children and a godly wife, I did not see my life progressing as I had intended. I felt like I had no balance around me or even in my head. God began to speak to me. I realized the reason I was struggling was because I had picked up unhealthy habits, some of which came from where I was in my life. I was dealing with the recent losses of family members and the state of where the world was concerning covid. I realized all of these issues affected my mental health and I needed to have some sort of healthy balance. I had also picked up unhealthy relationship habits. Some things were obvious, and some were not. For example, I picked up a habit of procrastinating and was delaying the things that I needed to take care of. I was at a place of complacency, and change needed to happen right away.

There were things that God was telling me to birth, but I couldn't because I was mentally exhausted. I started making a habit of letting stuff go that needed to be addressed at that moment. One day I heard in my spirit, "Make room." I kept hearing it. I began to give away clothes, jewelry, and shoes. I began to declutter my spirit and anything that was hindering my growth in the spirit and in the natural. I realized that all of those unhealthy habits were making my lifestyle unhealthy. I am grateful to God for showing me the habits that were corrupting my life.

Self-Love

The most powerful healing journey of the self-love process is understanding authentic love and that I am well deserving of receiving love authentically. I learned to embrace my scars and love me and my imperfections. I understood God's love for me and what is not love. Another powerful revelation was knowing I did not have to sit in the presence of people who did not celebrate me, but only tolerated me. I know life comes with many oppositions and everything is not going to be perfect, but there are believers that do have the heart of Christ and will love you with the heart of Christ. I have the right to be in the presence of people that are assigned to my life. I had struggled in the love area, so God showed me what love was when I was in my sinful state. God loved me and pulled me through every trial. I found love in Jesus Christ. I was no longer seeking to find love and to fill any empty voids. I am God's daughter. Even though I was unworthy, God still loved me.

As a young girl, my mother would oftentimes tell me that I would not be whole until I no longer needed to be validated by men. She said, "Stop giving away your power to people who don't have a heaven or hell for you." I remember the conversation like it was yesterday. I learned that I was wonderfully made by God and everyone was not a part of my tribe. Who God had for me was for me. It felt so good to live my life unapologetically. I learned to live my life on purpose. When I used to get attacked I would get bent out of shape about who, why and what was said. But God reminded me of his word and what I was called to do.

I admired my mother because she had such a bold and courageous spirit, and yet I was so shy and timid. I was a woman dealing with my inner child and allowing God to give me a bold spirit. God started to bring the boldness out of me. Before I never really liked dealing with confrontation. I would usually walk away because I was so focused on how people would view me after confronting a situation. For instance, I had a disagreement with one of my closest friends. I hung up the phone and assumed that the disagreement was over. God told me, "No. Call her back and deal with that disagreement." I realized at that moment I had the right to speak up about my feelings and the actions that were done to me irresponsibly. I learned the importance of dealing with issues so that they don't become built up offenses.

Another powerful lesson was that I had to unlearn some unhealthy cycles and limited beliefs, knowing that everyone doesn't have the same story. It was important not to allow everyone to insert their view into my life. I was to listen clearly to God's voice for clarity for my entire life.

I had to learn how to disconnect myself from unhealthy connections and relationships. I realized I needed healing in this area. I would oftentimes refer back to what was and if it was comfortable to me. I had to learn how important it was to let go of that unhealthy habit. I walked away from things God told me to walk away from. One day while riding home from church I was having a conversation with my middle child Reny concerning her past experience as a child. She told me, "Mom, I wish I could have been embraced by people who were in leadership and could have helped me understand my gifts. Maybe they could have helped nurture me and train me in my gifts."

At that moment I realized that all my children may have dealt with some abuse in leadership just like me. I looked at my daughter and said, "I'm sorry daughter for what I allowed when I was broken." At that point, I understood about breaking generational cycles, as a mother, by apologizing to my child. I understood that not only was mental health important, but spiritual health matters. Although oppositions do happen in the life of a believer, you have to know when to walk away from connections that are not God ordained. Even in my relationship patterns I would go back to what seemed safe and comfortable to me. Every time I broke up from a relationship, that ex-boyfriend would come back out of nowhere with those familiar spirits. I had to learn to shut the door to the past for good and move forward.

Everybody Is Not My Assignment

When you have a caregiver nature you allow yourself to carry people's burdens, responsibilities, and baggage. This describes me. Even as a little girl, I was always taking on people's responsibilities. As a believer I felt I was doing a good deed and being a good Samaritan, but I had no boundaries, no cut off point. Even the people I helped, manipulated me with wrong motives and intentions. I found myself getting burned out and really drained. Because I was a giver and sower, not only monetary, but with my time, sometimes it caused an unhealthy balance in my household. But I felt that if nobody else did it, then I had to step in and make it happen. When I was married it caused friction in the home and sometimes that meant my children's meal time was pushed back.

What really bothered me at the time was the slander and the cursing that came behind the help I gave, and that really hurt. My intentions were to be a blessing, but it turned into a mess. I had to really dig deep to find out where the behavior came from. I realized I was following the examples

119

of my grandma. I watched her go above and beyond for her family, always available to be there for anyone. But I never saw the balance. I watched my mother follow the same pattern. My mother was definitely her family's caregiver, and growing up, my siblings and I would get angry because of the many sacrifices that she made for family members. Not to mention, my mother had health problems herself. I watched my mom put her life on hold to help take care of her mom and sister until God called them home. There was never a level of honor and respect for her. Sometimes a person can continue in the same cycle for so long and not know how to really change that pattern. So, I had to not only set the boundaries for myself, but my mom as well. I could no longer carry other people's weight. I had to examine the possibilities that the spirit of rejection and abandonment were operating. I was an overdoer. I made sure that everyone was happy even when I was left exhausted. I had to learn the power of no. Also, healthy boundaries were a part of my self-love. Whoever was in my life had to respect those boundaries.

CHAPTER 29

Overcoming Rejection And Abandonment

A S A CHILD, I WAS ALWAYS RESENTED AND DESPISED BY MY FAMILY members because they were envious of my life. I grew up blessed with food, shelter, and love. I was persecuted for an upbringing that I had no control over.

Growing up, I embraced rejection so much that I hid in the shadows running away from my calling. I had so much potential and gifts that God placed inside of me, but rejection showed up in every area of my life. Therefore, I was stuck in bitterness and repeated scenarios that played in my mind. I was unable to grow in life and really live a healthy life. Living in fear of abandonment and rejection made me become cautious about who I allowed in my space. I kept up a defense against people I was really afraid, at times, to let people in. I was walking in hurt and in a place of offense. There were times where unforgiveness would creep in me and I had no clue. As a believer I had to forgive the people that did not want to build a relationship with me and continually walked out of my life. I was confused because the love that I gave was not the love that was reciprocated. There were times when I felt worthless, and other times I felt like I deserved better. I remember relieving myself of the responsibility of carrying the burden of being rejected and abandoned knowing it wasn't my fault, and learning how to be vulnerable enough to deal with the emotions that came behind those spirits. It was beyond my control. Some of the occurrences happened when I was a child. As a child, naturally when you are rejected you think there's something wrong with you. As an adult, I realized those were unhealed wounds.

I became a busybody. Everything was about work. I started to isolate myself from crowds because of fear of not being accepted and because of my awkward behavior in unhealthy environments. God had to teach me how to love my brothers and sisters in Christ, but also when it's time to leave an environment in a healthy way. Even in my unhealed places in my life, I realized that God was calling me to the broken hearted, rejected, and outcast. My vision became so clear once God showed me who I was. I remember owning and walking in my truth. I had the audacity to become better step by step and I understood every step was to be celebrated.

I realized there were so many, who struggled with the same issues, that were drawn to me because they needed healing. God had given me a heart of compassion and he was going to use me to minister to a broken generation. As God revealed to me that he wanted me to be whole, I realized it was my responsibility to allow God to heal me, but I had to believe and obey his strategies. I understood that everything I had been through was part of God's plan to launch me forward in him.

As a young lady, I can recall going into different environments and different rooms where I was rejected, maybe because of status, material possessions, or even physical appearance. Experiencing those same feelings as a grown woman was different because of the revelation that God had given me. When I was younger I was unable to identify who I was in God and to differentiate those emotions and not allow them to deter me from my God-given purpose. I wasn't good enough for some people but I was good enough for God. God showed me so many times how valuable I am to him. I realized that I am not called to everybody and I started to understand that. I am God's elected and called, and I walk proudly with assurance of who I am in God.

I am called to a generation, and everybody is not a part of that generation. I had to learn to be okay with that reality. I experienced rejection so severe that I stayed in spiritual caves and called it separation, but instead I was having crying spells in repetitive cycles. I was unable to break free because I was embracing it instead of facing rejection and my insecurities.

I knew what the bible said about forgiveness, but oftentimes it was easier said than done. I recall many times when I was rejected in relationships and friendships. I could not connect with people because of my suspicions and uneasiness. Rejection can consume your life on so many levels, especially when God is connecting you with people that are aligned to your destiny. I dealt with so many cycles of rejections for many years. However, I realized that trouble doesn't last always. God knew that I wanted to be free from this spirit. I was able to face my reality while desperately praying and asking Jesus to deliver me from this spirit that was having my life shipwrecked. I wanted to walk in the peace of God and be the woman that I knew God wanted me to be. I remember praying to God before about rejection in my past, but this time was different. I logged on to Facebook one day, and a Prophetess, who was on the live, gave me a powerful word directly from God. "God is raising you to be a great leader in him. You will begin to speak with power and authority where people will ask who you are with such authority and a deeper level of teaching. I see you feel like your cross is heavy. Hold on. God said, 'Get over your offenses with people.' There were some people that showed you their character and revealed their heart, but stay focused because God is going to exalt you for his glory. I see you teaching the youth with such power and authority."

The more I spent time with God the more I felt free. I was not worrying about who misunderstood me, or who did not like me. I was free from any shame that the enemy tried to hold over me. I now walk with purpose holding my head up high knowing I am a daughter of the king.

CHAPTER 30

God Revealing My Friendships/ Relationships

I N PRAYER I ASKED GOD TO SHOW ME MY CONNECTIONS. THERE WERE some people that God showed me that he was blocking from my life. I have always been a person that loved hard and was a very supportive person. I looked at my friends as family because I didn't have a healthy relationship with my own family. In my past, I really dealt with a lot of people who were not genuine. So, my buddies were family to me. Meanwhile the older I got, I started seeing things in friendships that I did not like. Around 2017, it was more obvious that I had some of the wrong connections. It was a feeling I had in the presence of some of my friends. I prayed and asked God to show me who was connected to my future.

I had to cut some people off that were draining my spirit. We were on different pages with different mindsets. My growth started to annoy the people that were in a place of complacency. Their unhealthy qualities were different from mine which caused friction in our friendships and relationships. I was walking in a different direction, and staying connected would have hindered my walk with Christ. I broke generational cycles, so some repeated experiences were no longer welcomed.

Oftentimes, I expected the people I had been rocking with for many years to be the ones supporting and rooting for me, but sometimes the people that you meet later can add so much value to your life. Sometimes you must be careful about what you ask God for because he will show you, but you have to be prepared for what God shows you. In three dreams,

God showed me people that did not have my best interest at heart. When I tell you, it hurt. Because I loved with the love of God, it was hard for me to digest the truth of what God showed me. However, because of maturity in God my response was different. The old me would have been upset and offended, but the growth was necessary for the new level that God was taking me to. When they say, "Old ways won't open new doors," please believe it. I used my energy to pray for my enemies and realized that people hated on me because they hated something about themselves that they were not healed from. I had to understand that because I needed to feel accepted, I was willing to tolerate unhealthy relationships by giving people access to me that God never gave me permission to give. Even in the midst of the people that started to fall off, I learned to be loyal to God, not people. Man will fail you, but God will never fail you. People that truly love you want you to succeed in your life in all areas. True friends and family help support, promote, and sometimes build with you.

I remember when people started shedding from my life. In the beginning I was hurt, but God was exposing their hearts and my heart. He was showing me that some friendships I thought I had had not been beneficial. God was testing my heart by showing me, and I realized that I was not to change my heart posture. I had to be okay with releasing myself from toxic relationships and walk away without feeling bad for doing it. My life had consisted of being connected to toxic people with the wrong intentions. So as God showed me the hearts and characters of the people that I was connected to, I was okay with walking away. Whether it's a parent that doesn't want to step up and play an appropriate role in your life, friendships, or relationships, you cannot force people to stay in your life. Instead, I learned to value the people that added value to my life.

CHAPTER 31

Seeking God For Wholeness

AN YOU IMAGINE SEEKING FOR SOMETHING THAT IS REAL? GROWING up, what appeared to be real was counterfeit. I desired real connections and real love from the people that were supposed to be authentic. I was struggling and began to ask God to show me genuine relationships and connections. There were broken pieces inside of me with some unanswered questions. I would oftentimes ask God why and then answer the same question when I realized what Jesus endured on earth. The broken relationships and unhealthy connections caused me to go into a depression. It was those moments in the bed at night that I was crying sometimes until my pillow was soaked. Although I knew how to mask well, some days people knew I was struggling. One thing for sure, true believers in Christ knew I was struggling.

I remember sometimes battling so bad that I would tell my husband, "Babe please pray for me." I felt like I could not make it through the mind battles that I was struggling with. I was in the fight of my life in all areas. Sometimes I did not feel like fighting with the world when I had to fight everyday not to become depressed. It is never a funny situation at all when one of your own is struggling with these same battles. I told God that I was tired of dealing with warfare. It was not until I was so tired of dealing with depression that the Lord allowed me to understand that I had Jesus and therapy and to not be ashamed. I knew the power of prayer and I knew that the only way that this depression would break off my life was with prayer, fasting, support, and therapy. I asked myself, "How does a child who came into the world as a happy child now struggle with depression?" It's so easy.

Dealing with life in general is a lot and every individual processes their pain differently. I also realized that I had been through a lot of things that some people would probably commit suicide over.

I remember feeling alone having no one to talk to about my inner struggles and emotions. It seemed like almost everyone around me needed to be encouraged and empowered. The question crossed my mind, "Who can pray for me through the tough times when I am going through?" I felt like that often. I realized that I could not keep pouring from an empty cup. I had to learn to make adjustments. One day I began to cry out and to pray to God. At that moment I felt something break off of me. I was on the road of recovery to healing. I told myself, "Whatever it takes and however long it takes, I will walk in healing and wholeness in God. No longer will I stay in bondage to my past or to any generational curses, curse words or life trauma!" I realized God wanted me to let go of all the baggage that I was carrying because it did not belong to me anyway. I must take back my power as the woman that God had called me to be. I would no longer live my life in the past. That day I was living for my future. I had lived my life in the past and allowed myself to bandage and mask my pain instead of dealing with the reality of what was going on. Self-awareness was especially important to me in this season because instead of living life as normal, taking care of everyone around me, I had to learn to take care of myself.

One day while going to a training, I was in a car accident that could have cost me my life, but God spared me. My life changed completely at that moment. God spoke to me, "I am your God, your keeper." I began to weep because God reassured me that he protected me and he had work for me to do. My lifestyle was altered. I had to make major adjustments while I was in the healing process. I was forced again to focus on myself. My chiropractor dropped some nuggets on me when I went to my apartment. He told me, "Love, my mother once told me God loves people who take care of themselves. If you can't take care of yourself, how can you take care of God's people?" I thought about what was communicated to me. I had to declutter my mind to receive this reality that self-love was important to God and to never forget it. My whole mindset shifted. I started looking at my life from a different perspective and neglecting myself was draining me. I started implementing self-care at home and it started to be a lifestyle.

CHAPTER 32

Learning How To Release
People And The Hurt

EARNING HOW TO RELEASE PEOPLE WAS EXTREMELY HARD. I HAD A co-dependency issue. I had a need for friends, family, and relationships because of fear of being abandoned again. I was still that rejected little girl in an adult form. Although I was grown, I still had those painful wounds.

I remember listening to a bishop on YouTube when he talked about the gift of goodbye. The message really showed me why it was important to release myself from unhealthy connections. I did not get it in the beginning because I felt like I needed some people in my circle. But God started revealing the characters and hearts of the people that I was connected to. I knew at that point that I had to make some adjustments. I knew I had to shed off those toxic relationships. That was the hardest decision that I had to make, because oftentimes, I didn't realize that the connections were a toxic cycle.

I found myself staying in places too long. God had to show me that he had someone assigned to my destiny that was going to add value to my life. I told myself that I would no longer hold onto forced relationships or be in environments that were unhealthy for me and my children. I realized I could leave any situation or connection that God was telling me to move on from. God taught me that it's okay to leave, but it's how you leave. You can use wisdom and leave healed and not be bitter. I realized that we put other people's feelings over God. God can tell you to leave a place, but you do not because you are worrying about people's feelings instead of obeying God. Whether it is relationships, friendships, or environments, if God tells you to leave, do it in peace. Obey God over man. Do not be a pleaser of man, if so, you are not worthy of the Father.

I remember seeing how affected my children were concerning the people that I had to leave in my past. You'd be surprised to know how much growing children can identify what is going on and have their own perspective on bad connections. I had to challenge my children to look at things from a different perspective. I taught my children to appreciate the people that God called to their lives. As soon as I released some of those bad connections, I linked up with a network of trailblazers that were about their father's business: bosses, authors, entrepreneurs and career-oriented women. I remembered dreaming about major connections that were about to happen in my life. One day, a prophet came up to me and gave me a mighty word from God concerning my life. She gave me answers to the dreams that God was showing me. That prophetess blew my mind! I was so grateful that God was giving me another turn around. The Lord would show me so much and my pastor knew I had prophetic dreams. He used to say, "Isn't that right, Love?" I would agree oftentimes because I was literally hearing and seeing what God was revealing.

The ministry was made up of majority women, but the lack of love for each other was disheartening. The church transitioned many times but, with the last crew it was harder to get everyone to come together on one accord. I was mislabeled and judged because many people thought I was single, but I was married with three children. It wasn't until years later that I divorced. There is a stereotype in the church concerning unmarried women. It's like a discarded unworthy stigma put on singles. I remember when people found out that my husband and I were dating, I was attacked and slandered by a group of ladies. The slander went on for months because he proposed to me and a year later, we got married. Like some of those ladies in the ministry, there were other people who had their perceptions of who I was. My family had such a reputation that they felt like we were all fighters, thugs, alcoholics, weed heads, and nobodies.

There was one lady in particular that joined the church and later on married my cousin. I knew from the beginning that I was not liked by her because God showed me. Out of all of my cousin's relationships, she was the only one that I did not connect with. My children felt the same way. My daughters came to me one day and told me that my cousin's stepsons tried to belittle them by calling them ghetto. Later on, my son started dating the daughter of my daughter's praise dance teacher, and he was looked down on as not being good enough. I began to get so furious about what was happening and lashed out. I was tired of the ongoing drama towards me and my children.

With all the turmoil going on, the Lord was showing me that my season was up at that church, but I continued to stay anyway. I came into the ministry at the age of 23 and I was well invested in the ministry. I wanted to be faithful unto God and do his will. God had called me to teach the youth, but the leadership blocked me every time. My pastor, who was sick at the time, would tell me to teach the youth, but the first lady and my cousin-in-law continually blocked me from doing what God said.

One day another woman was having a problem with this same deaconess, and she reached out to me. I tried to be a peacemaker and told her to go to her and have a conversation. Prior to this day the Lord had shown me snakes in my inner circle. I had no clue what I was about to go through and that I was being plotted against in this situation. That Sunday after church service, I was called into a meeting that had nothing to do with me. There was tension with the other women. I knew some of the women did not like me or half the time didn't speak to me. Although I was okay just giving it to God and allowing him to deal with it, I had to continually deal with jabs. At this point with everything that was going on, I was definitely provoked.

I can be in a crowd of people who do not like me and still show love, but I was out of character in that meeting because I was tired and I felt my back was against the wall. No one was fighting for me but God. My children were getting older. I believe my son was about 17 years old and my daughters could have been 11 and 12. My son was so angry to see how ministries should not be done. Even in his early age he had already seen enough. It really hindered him from going back to church. I thought I was teaching my children to remain faithful, but instead I was teaching them to stay connected to unhealthy and toxic environments. I knew God was telling me to leave these people that misrepresented his image with all of the unforgiveness, shunning, plotting, and lies.

God said enough was enough. I was broken. Though these people had been like family to me, they did not forgive me for stepping out of character. I gravitated to my old nature that God had delivered me from. The hurt ran deep. My husband did not stand with me. I was on my own. I will admit that I told a lie because I didn't want to expose another person's truth. But I didn't understand why these believers didn't extend me the same grace they extended others in the ministry. I was only trying to protect another church member's reputation. I never even told my side of the story. I allowed myself to be looked at as the bad person because of the turmoil, and the pain that ran so deep in my heart. I knew this wasn't family. There were people that were over ministries who were gambling, fornicating, and using alcohol and drugs, yet they were forgiven.

Before I was uprooted from the ministry, the pastor called me and told me that she wanted my mother Evangelist Constance and myself to teach the youth. She taught the youth and I taught the teens. Whenever we taught the young people, they were excited to come to church. God moved every time, but once we stopped teaching my children didn't even want to come to church. My pastor friend was also here from Orlando, Florida, and we had kingdom enrichment that day. As I began to tell my mother what the pastor told us to do, she had a resistance that rose up in her. She said she was not led to teach. I told her that we had permission from the pastor.

That same day after my mom and I taught, a couple of leaders came to us saying we weren't supposed to be teaching and this was the first lady's instructions. We were humiliated and my spirit was crushed. My pastor friend from Orlando, Florida looked at me and my mom and then said to everyone that we all needed to be on one accord. My brother Elder Joe, who always spoke life into me and my children, saw spiritually through all of the confusion. As we went outside and got into the car, Elder saw the hurt and he tried to cheer my mom and me up. I never got a chance to thank him. Because of him remaining in God's image I knew I could heal from this level of pain and abuse from leadership. I walked away afraid of what was going to be said about me, and I was right. There were rumors!

A great lesson I learned from all of this is that prayer is the key. Learning to forgive quickly is vital. At the time, all I saw was the enemy that was fighting against me, not understanding that prayer and the word of God are my weapons.

In reality, you can become so blind in leadership that you walk in the spirit of error. God told me personally that some of the things that were going on in the ministry were not of him. I was told to leave but I stayed too long because we had a great outreach ministry that I was drawn to. In a dream, God showed me the leadership torn down. When I saw it I instantly started praying. The ministry was no longer, the sheep were scattered and bitter, and some did not return to ministry. Some just visited other churches. I walked away broken and many nights I cried myself to sleep.

Ministry was always a big part of my culture. I was all in, so the abuse really took a toll on me, but God healed me. I even went out to lunch with some of the old members. After what I experienced, however, I changed my whole circle. I realized giving grace and praying for them was what God instructed me to do. I also knew not to restore any relationship with anyone that did not love authentically. I couldn't be concerned about what people said or felt about me.

I had to release myself from the false expectations that people placed on me. I was yoked up with some unhealthy relationships and cycles. I had to deal with the hurt and release it so that I could move on in God. I could not continue to operate in the spirit of offense which was hindering my praise and worship unto God. If I did something wrong, I would instantly make it right because conviction would come over me so heavy. I couldn't hold onto a grudge or any form of unforgiveness. God was in control.

I realized the brokenness in me attracted brokenness in other people, whether they were relationships or friendships. The phrase "Hurt people hurt people" is an appropriate statement. Oftentimes I found myself being there for people who afflicted their pain and insecurities onto me. I was a caregiver before I realized I was always trying to fix people's lives. I was just pouring into the lives of others even when I felt depleted. I was an encourager by nature and I knew God had given me the gift to encourage and help shift mindsets, even though I was broken inside.

Self-reflection is so powerful because it has allowed me to identify my own imperfections. There were several times in my life where I saw warning signs about people that I was connected to. There were people that were sent into my life to deter me from my purpose, and others came into my life to add value to my life. However, I could not at the time distinguish the two because of all the unhealthy cycles and relationships I had experienced that were detrimental to my growth and development. I had held onto unhealthy things in my life for too long untill realized that part of my mental health was to stand up to the people that brought me down and tried to devalue my worth. When you have a heart of love you cannot allow everyone to have access to you. You cannot allow your purpose to be linked up with ungodly connections. I was tired of living in bondage and perpetuating pain, hurt, unforgiveness, and cycles. Life was too short to waste time on people that did not value or respect me as an individual. I really wanted to fully heal. I was tired of masking. I remember telling God, "No makeup or a smile God, I need you." There were some roots that had been planted from seeds that had grown that needed to be cut. I was desperate for healing because I realized this cycle had dominion over my life. Now it was time for change.

During the pain that I was experiencing, God gave me a women's ministry. I was usually a very shy person, except when I prayed. There was a level of boldness that came out of me when I prayed. I knew it was the Holy Spirit. One night I had a dream where I saw women experiencing the same pain I have experienced in my life, and they were crying out. It was a group of women. They were suffering and needed Jesus for a breakthrough. In the dream I could actually feel the pain. Since I was on the intercessory team, I told the elder that was over the team about my dream and she began to give me insight about the dream. The next week I was on the phone with my best friend praying and talking about the goodness of God. She began to give me a prophetic word from God saying, "The Lord said he is giving you a women's ministry and you are going to minister and encourage women, including influential women. I see you in auditoriums and coliseums. This ministry God gave to you. Just know when God calls you everyone is not going to accept the call." This word from my sister in Christ was confirmation about the dream and clarity of what God was calling me forth to do.

God has a sense of humor. Even in the midst of the turmoil, he was giving me a women's ministry. He had given me a heart and compassion for people. I recalled a time when I was 19 years old and my auntie told me,

"Nothing will go right until you do what God called you to do." I looked at my aunt and said, "Not me." I was not ready to carry a mantle. I felt like my cross was already heavy. I wanted to live a simple life. However, I realized that I was marked. I just did not want to walk in the shoes of my family. It seemed like there was already a lot of pressure because of the call, but my family was chosen. It had been prophesied about since I was a little girl,but I still did not want that pressure. My mother had the fivefold ministries in her, so I felt like people were pressuring me because of my lineage.

Sometimes surrendering is easier said than done. You must be prepared for what comes along with accepting Christ as your personal savior. I started rejecting who I was because I never felt worthy of the call. Matter fact, I realized that every day I am a filthy rag only used by God.

Sometimes letting go of people that God is calling you away from can be hard because you hold onto the memories and history of who they used to be. As people we change from day to day. I can recall some friendships that were great in the past, but then we grew apart in the future. We have to get over the perception that people will have a heart like yours. I remember a prophet told me, "You have been around people that had bad character and God showed you who they were. Stay the course because God wants to raise you up to be a great leader in the kingdom." That word was right on time.

I almost gave up on the building that I fellowshipped in because I wanted to see the true church. I told God that I was tired and did not want to be around anyone that did not have a heart of love for me. I was tired of loving people that I knew did not like me. So, I started separating myself from people. I was tired. I stopped going to church. I mean I stopped reading my word, praying, etc. My teenage son at the time asked me, "Mom, what's going on? I miss the mother who was anchored in God." I realized I was on my way back to the old me. So, God sent a prophet in my dream to give me a word. She told me everything I was doing and said, "God says it's time to get back on course."

Understanding where I was spiritually, Satan's job was to put me back in the mindset of pain. But God did a quick work in me. God has matured me in levels that some people must grow to. God started giving me bible scriptures to get over my trials. I had to refocus my mindset to keep my mind on Christ and not on the enemy that comes against me.

After the suffering of childhood trauma, pain, and many life disappointments, the Rescuer Jesus Christ rescued me from a desolate place. I felt hopeless and was ready to give up on my assignment and on myself. I had no confidence in what God was calling me to do. I was damaged and my God came right on time and gave me purpose and a reason to live and belong. God assured me that I was a part of his plan. God was even equipping me and building my character to spread the gospel of Jesus Christ. I was now in a season of my life where God was my priority.

CHAPTER 33

I Am A Curse Breaker

GENERATIONAL CURSES AND ANCIENT RULINGS ARE SO POWERFUL AND can have demonic influences over your present and future if you don't denounce or break demonic agreements. As an intercessor, God revealed to me specifically how I should pray. After revelation of the curses that were operating over my family, I began to denounce depression, alcoholism, witchcraft, and generational sins. I continued to pray and declare blessings. I declared, "I am the righteousness of Christ. My family is healed and set free from any deeply rooted sin. We are free in Jesus Christ." After declaring God's word, I continued to stand in the gap for my family, breaking generational cycles in our spiritual walk and in our everyday lifestyles and rebuking every unclean spirit.

The obvious cycles that were in our family were slander, competition, gossip, backbiting, and jealousy. The older I got I wanted to bring my children around so they could get a little different experience concerning family. I realized that some things had changed. I had to continue to be the change I wanted to see. Breaking through barriers while setting boundaries, I taught my children to love everyone.

Creating a new family dynamic was very important to me. As a woman with three children, I learned to unlearn some old patterns and worldly systems. I adopted a different dynamic for my household. God taught me how not to pass down past unhealthy generational cycles. When it comes to my old nature and traditional cycles I have unlearned old habits and behaviors. There were some generational cycles, and worldly traditions that I had to overthrow because it was detrimental to my growth. I did not want my children to experience the same trauma. I wanted something different. I wanted a sense of normalcy. Some spirits I had to denounce were the spirits of jealousy, competition, and slander. These spirits were really major in my family. I had to demolish these spirits so that I did not pass it down to my children.

With prayer and God's word, the Holy Spirit taught and matured me so that I would have the capacity to teach my children from a biblical standpoint. My decisions were no longer influenced by what I was taught that was unhealthy, but by the teachings that were biblical and true. Some things I continued to hold on to were seeds that were planted by my mother, grandmother, and other spiritual influencers that God had placed in my life.

I found myself speaking life into my children's lives daily and building their self-esteem and confidence, which allowed them to understand that they don't ever have to compete with anyone, but just be original, different, and unique. They were taught not to be people pleasers, but who God created them to be. I had to heal so that my children would not have to receive that unhealed version of their mother. With much preparation, God allowed me to see how important it was to have a transformed mind concerning my outlook on life. Adapting to a new way of living was powerful and purposeful. I don't have to despise my upbringing because it helped shape my new viewpoint of life. I had to allow my children to be who God created them to be instead of trying to live my life through them. As a parent, I would see the giftings in my children and nurture and pull them out of them.

No, I am not perfect, and neither are my children, in spite of the constant rumors that spread amongst the family that I put my children on a pedestal. In reality, I encouraged, uplifted, and disciplined them. Every time I had to discipline them it was a teaching moment so that they understood the reason why.

I unapologetically began to shed off the worldly patterns that weren't pleasing to God. I was creating a legacy for my family and for the next generation. I did not want a way of life that would cause emotional damage to myself and my children. For instance, I began to make my own family events, and I chose not to spend a whole lot of money for Christmas. I did not have to worry about men's condemnation because I found true fulfillment in God and my immediate family instead of monetary gifts.

CHAPTER 34

The Power Of Planted Seeds

PLANTING SEEDS IS POWERFUL. THERE IS A PROCESS THAT HAS TO happen. The same time that you plant seeds is not the same time you receive a harvest. As a young girl, those godly principles that were planted on the inside of me were not in vain. There was an appointed time to see the fruits of the seeds planted in my life.

There were many powerful women that God placed in my life. Some were just passing through my life, while others left a powerful imprint on my heart. Not to mention, I was able to identify what a sonship and a bastard child are. As a woman who did not have a close father connection growing up, my former pastor exemplified what a spiritual father is and the characteristics that a man should have.

My grandma played a very important role model in my life. She played a very powerful influential role in my life by her lifestyle, conduct, and love language. She planted so many powerful seeds in life concerning being a believer and also how to co-exist in society. She introduced her children to God, and my mother introduced me to God. Being taught about generational blessings was the most powerful biblical teaching that I was ever given. When Mom was in a backslidden state, I was still able to look at godly examples from my grandmother. Even today as a modern woman, I've learned so many things that I have passed down to my children. I have learned spiritual principles about God and practical living. Reading God's word and receiving revelation of God during studying and praying has helped me grow in God. Growing from a child into a woman, I have learned how to put God first in my life, have a personal relationship with

God and be a good steward over my finances. The balance of how to live a spiritual life in a natural world is vitally important. There were certain things, words of affirmation, and words of life that helped set me on fire to thrive in life and to be who God wants me to be. I recall my mother telling me in my teenage years, "You can be whatever you want to be in life, and you don't need permission to do it." This powerful word has helped shape my mindset throughout life.

My spiritual mother took me in spiritually as a real daughter and helped groom me in my spiritual journey with Christ. There was so much the Lord revealed to her about me. The more I grew in God, the more I discovered the many giftings that God placed inside of me.

When I was about 24 years old, my pastor, who was a tall stern man with a squeaky voice, was so adamant about teaching women how to not settle for the wrong men and to better themselves. As a young woman with daddy issues, I remember being attentive to his powerful messages. Not that he did not pour into the men, but the culture of women was well in need. In modern society, women now outnumber men in the church. It was my pastor who helped show me what it is to have a father, and what a husband is. My mother wasn't married so the only example I saw was how he treated his wife. That example taught me what I needed to see concerning having a healthy godly relationship. God knew exactly who and what I needed to help me grow in my spiritual journey in life. The many attributes from early connections are what helped mold me into the mature woman that God intended me to be.

CHAPTER 35

God My Miracle Worker And Protector

I HAVE HAD SEVERAL NEAR-DEATH EXPERIENCES IN MY LIFE. WHEN I was 19 years old, death was so close to me, and that's when I realized that God was with me. One day I went to a fish bar downtown on Race Street and hesitated to get out of the car to go purchase the fish dinners. As my mom repeatedly told me to go, I looked for a parking spot and proceeded to get out of the car along with my aunt Cookie and my 3-year-old son. As we began to walk, a guy walked directly behind us while my mother was in the car. My mother said as she glanced at him, she saw a demon. As we were walking, bullets started flying past us, but God kept us. To witness murder and to see rage in the murderer's eyes was so scary. The police authorities were so amazed by how we weren't shot or grazed. This was yet another miracle where God kept me. On another day, when I was leaving college God delayed my bus, and as soon as the bus reached my destination, I saw a young male face forward dead in a puddle of blood. I knew if my bus had come on time I could have been in a crossfire, but God kept me. God is my protector and I am grateful that I did not lose my life prematurely.

By just living, I realized that God is a miracle worker. I have so many testimonies on the miraculous things that God has done in my life. When I think about Jesus Christ himself being the ultimate miracle to all mankind, Christ's plan of salvation was enough for me to be forever indebted to God. Many moments in my life, God has proven himself to me to be a promise keeper. God has given me instant miracles and three-day miracles. I realized even as a child growing up that God dealt with me concerning the number 3. Miracles happened for me in three days, and I was delivered from smoking cigarettes within three days at the age of 23. After praying and crying out to God with a close friend, God spoke through my friend Trina, "If you continue to seek me, I will take the taste of cigarettes from your tastes buds." And on the third day I did not have a desire nor was I addicted to cigarettes anymore. I began to rejoice again because the Lord had done it again.

I must brag about how God has come through for me over and over again. After Mom delivered me in the hospital and after hearing news that I wasn't going to make it, God had other plans for my life. Even after rebelling against God by getting pregnant in the church out of wedlock and having my son prematurely, God spoke to me at that moment and said, "He's going to make it". I had that assurance because I knew God spoke it and it was so.

At the age of 19 I was extremely sick and dealing with painful back pains. Unable to eat, I spent time with God in prayer and cried out to him. I was so sick I didn't think I was going to make it. God spoke to me in a still voice, "On the third day I will remove the pain from your back." On the third day I did not feel any pain. I began to weep because I knew that God did yet another miracle once again. There was a time when God would speak to me clearly and I knew it was him speaking because God watches over his word and his word cannot come back to him void.

I remember yet another miracle when I was in college and God was superseding my expectations. I was praying for a home in an area that people swore I wasn't going to get. And I was in college struggling with a class that I needed to pass in order to graduate from college. As I went to the bathroom during class, I asked God for a miracle, without my faith wavering. God responded to my prayer right away. I received a call approving me for the house I applied for and I was so excited! I went back to class to take my test and, instantly, I tested out of the class having the highest score in the class. I prayed and asked for a miracle and God gave me a double miracle.

All through my life I've watched the hand of God on my life. How wonderful it is for a daughter to be loved by her heavenly father who is concerned with things that concern her! I remember so vividly how my grandma emphasized the importance of having a personal relationship with God by spending time with God, reading his word, praying to him and believing that he is going to perform it. Throughout my journey, prayer has been my posture, and having faith was vital. Prayer and faith are a powerful combination that activates miracles. My prayer has always been: "Lord reveal yourself to me so that I know that you are God." The power of God is limitless, uncaged and bigger than man's comprehension.

CHAPTER 36

Dealing With Grief And Loss

L IFE HAS TAUGHT ME THAT GRIEF COMES FROM SO MANY DIFFERENT categories of your life, not just death. Oftentimes grief comes from the loss of something. It can be a person, job, relationship, ect. Losing something can affect you in a major way. I remember feeling the pain of heartache after being married for 7 years and having to file for divorce. Losing this marriage was hard on me and my children because of the time invested. I had to alter my life, and not being able to adjust to the new role and lifestyle took a toll on me. It was the worst pain ever which affected part of me. So, we needed the right support team in order to help us through this loss.

I remember making really good money at a good company that promoted me to a higher position. I had worked for this company for many years and the coordinator offered me a higher position with a higher pay rate. I accepted the position and I was so happy that as a woman I was able to take care of my children, pay bills, and still have money available to spend or save. I was so grateful to be able to maintain that position for years until the company lost its contract, which changed my entire financial situation. I began to feel frustrated and eventually became depressed because of the loss.

Dealing with the loss of loved ones and friends isn't easy. From the time I was a young girl even until my adult age, I lost people that I was extremely close to. Oftentimes as a child I really did not understand death and how to process the fact that the people that passed on would no longer be a part of my physical life. Throughout my life I made great connections, and so some hit me harder than others. Although my father wasn't present, my uncles were great male role models in my life. No, they weren't perfect, but they were the closest to a male figure that I could see. I remember the loss of some close family members that really affected me, and at one point I became depressed. I lost a close uncle at an early age, grandparents, and cousins that were like sisters and brothers to me. I lost a close prayer partner friend due to a brain tumor. She was a best friend of my close cousin, but when we met the God in us connected. I talked to my friend two weeks prior to her passing. Once again, my faith was really tested. I had questions in my heart concerning her sudden passing. This really messed me up. I felt like the ones that were close to me were leaving too soon. I was so broken and did not understand. I had to repent and ask God to strengthen me when I lost someone that was close to me.

I experienced major losses from several relatives, including aunts, cousins, and friends. My close male relative's death was so unexpected that it hit me really hard. I was in disbelief and I couldn't believe he was gone. I realized that the bond that we shared was valuable. The reality that he was gone didn't sit well with me. I was depressed and grieving at the same time even in the midst of a pandemic. I started to see behaviors in my teenage daughters that concerned me as a mother. With prayer and understanding I realized that it was okay to allow yourself to grieve and to take one day at a time and not allow people to put stipulations on your grieving process. God makes each individual different and it's okay to take a mental check evaluation.

I look at death and loss differently now. As I've matured in God, I understand that we are only here on God's time. God lends people to us. It's not permanent. Earth is temporary, but heaven is eternal. I am okay with what God is doing.

CHAPTER 37

There's Power In A Praying Woman

PRAYER IS A POWERFUL TOOL THAT I LEARNED HOW TO IMPLEMENT throughout my daily lifestyle. As a woman in Christ, I'm yet living life while facing many challenges, trials and tribulations through life's journey. Because of the magnitude of the trauma and pain I went through, I realized early on in life that prayer would help me navigate throughout my life. Prayer is a vital part of my life. And prayer changes things. Prayer is a powerful tool that allows me to communicate with Jesus Christ. I learned to pray for God's perfect will. Although I was taught how to pray at an early age, it wasn't until I got deep in the word of God when God showed me how to pray.

Prayer also helped me to develop a close and intimate relationship with God. I learned how to hear God's voice clearly and to surrender to his perfect will, so that he could bring me back in alignment with his divine purpose for my life. When I was a young girl learning the importance of prayer, oftentimes I did not know how to really articulate my words. I believe it was in my teenage years when I was taught the importance of prayer by the matriarch that God placed in my life. At 14 years of age is when I witnessed the power of prayer and how to respond when I pray. I remember crying out to God at the time. I needed guidance from God because I was going to make a decision concerning my future. God responded right away. It scared and shocked me, and at that moment I knew God was real. As I began to grow and mature in God, I realized that God responds to my prayers. I learned to be careful with what comes out of my mouth. Even in my tears and in the moments when I can't find the words to say, God is faithful. When I can't say a mumbling word, I know the Holy Spirit makes intercession for me.

When I was lost and needed guidance it was prayer that put me on the right path and gave me direction. Prayer shifted atmospheres and canceled out the enemy's assignments. No matter what situation that I was facing in life, whether good or uncomfortable, God would always bring me back to a place of prayer and repentance. Prayer helped me to be aligned with God's will. It was in prayer that I was able to feel God's presence.

The bible gives clear instructions on how to pray and that the prayers of the righteous avail much. Through prayer was where God moved and spoke to me and assured me as a young parent that my premature son was going to live. Through prayer and seeking God many times is where my deliverance took place. I remember so vividly when my car shut off on the road. I couldn't stop and was rolling down a hill in traffic. It was in prayer where God moved and protected me and my family from death.

As I began to grow in God, God called me to a higher level of prayer in him, not just a circumstantial prayer, but for prayer to be my posture consistently. Whether I am in the pit or in the palace, prayer should always be a part of who I am. When it was revealed that I was an intercessor God increased my capacity to war in the spirit. There were many mornings, usually around 3 am, when God would wake me up to pray for the nation. Even when I was feeling ungodly influences in the spiritual realm, God would give me that unction to pray a prayer of surrendering to God's will. Healing has taken place over the phone in the midst of prayer. I realized that, with the right motives, whatever I asked the father in Jesus' name, he would do it. God responded to my prayers. God is not slack concerning his promises. I realized I had to first believe in what God says. Even if I did not get what I prayed for, it does not mean God doesn't answer prayers. It just means it's all in God's timing, and maybe I have to reevaluate my prayers. The more I spent time with God praying and fasting, the more I realized my prayers should be in God's will, not my own. In my secret place I even wrote a prayer for hope and healing.

Prayer for Healing and Wholeness

"God, I need you. Thank you for sending your son Jesus Christ to the earth to give us the right to the tree of life. Lord, I love you and I cry out to you for healing and wholeness in all areas. Jesus, by your stripes I am healed. I come against every stronghold, every demonic force, and every curse word and generational curse that is in me or anything in my bloodline, that they are burned up by Holy Ghost fire. I am a child of the most high God. There is no other God before thee. Search my heart and know my heart. God, you have all power in your hands. Healing is my portion, and God you are a just and undefeated God. Lord you have complete reign over my life, my mind and my emotions, so that you will be glorified. Deliver me from men's validation and opinions of me and allow me God to already see myself healed. Lord, let me see myself the way you see me. Lord, I want to be free from the spirit of rejection and abandonment, so I can experience healthy relationships and friendships in my life. And this prayer is sealed in the name of Jesus."

CHAPTER 38

From Shame To Beauty

I REMEMBER THE DISAPPOINTMENTS I FELT FROM THE PAST DECISIONS I made as a woman who wasn't healed and who had been brought up in a single-parent home. Being wounded and having unhealed scars allowed me to make decisions that had consequences behind them. For instance, I used to despise my past decisions concerning getting pregnant early in the church at 16 years of age, which people still bring up today. But God, who is faithful and forgiving, looked beyond my faults and saw my needs. Now I smile because of the growth that God allowed me to experience. Being the topic of gossip, it wasn't easy growing up. But now I see how God meant it for my good.

One of my shameful moments was getting pregnant so young, unprepared, and scared. The gossip from the saints, friends, and family was embarrassing. I felt so ashamed because I knew better. However, there was so much perseverance and beauty that came out of my bad choice.

During my teenage years I started dating a guy who was in a gang. It seemed like I was attracted to bad boys, or thugs, as some people like to say. At the time I knew it wasn't a good look for me, but I loved the way he made me feel. He was two years older than me, but we seemed to get closer to each other. I was in love and I remember wanting to take the relationship to the next level. He then said, "Hold on, you clearly don't think we can go to the next level, do you? I love you babe, but I am a street guy and you are worth so much more, and I do not want to destroy your life." I didn't understand at the time, but later on I realized that he was telling the truth. Months later he got locked up and sent me a letter telling me how I would have had to be jumped in the game and be his gang queen. He told me, "I see much more in you young lady, like college, marriage, and business. Babe, my lifestyle will hinder your life and, as much as I love you, I can't walk away from this street lifestyle."

What was interesting was that it took someone who was living life foolishly to really see past what I saw. I saw failure and he saw purpose. I realized that because of my lack of love for myself and not being sure of myself, the need for validation and love was important to me. Even as a child growing up, I was insecure. I wondered why I would date such a guy who was in the streets, but I realized that he made me feel loved and safe.

Oftentimes I cried out to God and continued to replay scenarios in my head about the bad decisions I made. I didn't even consider that I was only human and that God had already forgiven me. It was people that held my past over my head. I had to learn how to move forward from the past and allow God to show me who I am in him.

After dealing with the consequences of the mistakes I made in life, I was forced to face my reality. I had been masking shame and humiliation for years. Sometimes it would show in my behavior. I would oftentimes hold my head down during conversations and feel inadequate as a woman. I had to choose to release myself from the burden of my past and allow God to teach me what real love is. I began to declare God's word over my life and affirm what God had already spoken to me. Many times, I would write down whatever God spoke to me as a reminder of what God said. God took my shame away.

I am now no longer bound to my past, but I am a new creature in God. As God's daughter God allowed his light to shine through me so that men would see his glory. There is beauty that comes out of the season of humiliation and shame, and that is learning how to remain faithful to God's will in the uncomfortable moments in life. My past no longer has power over me. I am now walking in double honor and in my purpose.

CHAPTER 39

A Woman Of Godly Influence

I REMEMBER NOT KNOWING THE POWER THAT I POSSESS, NOT BECAUSE of me, but because of the God that is within me. God has called me to do great work in the kingdom. I knew even as a child that God had blessed me with a unique purpose. I did not understand it in the beginning. I had to be broken from my own identity and agenda in order to see God's powerful plan of salvation. Even at the moments of my life when I felt unworthy and unqualified, God was doing miraculous things in my life. God was using me to go to places to pray for people, even when I had my own plans and agenda. God has qualified me, equipped me, and given me the Holy Spirit as leader and guide of all truth.

I am so grateful that God would oftentimes send me to places in twos. I recall a time when I went to the hairdresser, and my mom came along with me. As I walked into the stylist's home, I felt the spirit of heaviness and God placed it on my heart to pray for her. Before I asked the stylist if I could pray for her, my mother said, "The Lord said for you to pray." My mom's words of confirmation were teaching me more about when to know when God is speaking. So, I began to pray and I felt the atmosphere shift, and God moved in a mighty way. The following week, that same stylist called me and thanked me for praying for her, and I replied, "Don't thank me. Thank God." She proceeded to tell me that I confirmed everything when I was in prayer.

No matter how much I rebelled against God and ran from my calling, God chastised me and put me right back on track. It was time to obey God over man. As I got older, there was a greater level of surrendering to the will of God. I was no longer allowing fear to keep me stagnated. No longer would I allow my mouth to be muzzled by spiritual bullies. Although I wanted to walk away so many times and did not always obey God, he never took his hands off of me. He loved me with Agape love and looked beyond my faults and saw my needs. Scared, trembling and all, I gave God my yes! Since I am naturally an introvert, I had to learn how to adapt in environments where God was calling me to. My life was no longer mine.

Everything in my life has to glorify God, including my career and all my possessions. I have always said I don't want anything that takes me away from God. There are platforms, connections, and collaborations that I have to sometimes turn down because they misrepresent God. I must remove all fear and allow the spirit of boldness to rise up in me. When I open up my mouth God will speak through me. I am a woman of God who is on a mission with God's agenda to advance the kingdom of God. I am using my voice and platform to share the gospel all around the world.

CHAPTER 40

A Woman Of Beauty, Brains
And Creativity

A S A YOUNG GIRL, I GREW UP WATCHING MY MOTHER TAKE TIME AND interest in herself. Doing her hair and makeup and putting on fashionable clothing pieces, my mother was always making a statement with her creativity. My mom would always say, "Love, always make sure when you walk out the door to have yourself together. Make sure you are neat, clean and walk with confidence." So, when I showed up in the world it wasn't for attention or accolades, but it was a mother's gems being passed down to her daughter. Those same gifts of creativity my mother had passed down to me.

The older I got, I realized how I could apply my mom's teachings to my life. I also realized that God graced me with my own creativity and sense of fashion, and I had to recognize the many gifts and talents that he placed in me. The witty ideas God placed inside me were beyond my comprehension. For instance, I could walk in rooms that were bare, and I instantly would get a vision of how to execute designs in those rooms. God also blessed me with the gifts of beauty, event planning and music. Between my teenage and adult years, I wrote multiple songs. At 19 years old, I was on tv singing a song called "I Need You Lord," which I wrote after experiencing the trials of life. Singing and writing music was a way of escape for me. However, after having my son, I stopped working on music, and started focusing on raising my children.

Raising children caused me to put a lot of my goals on hold. I was in mommy mode a lot and so behind schedule. I started feeling unfulfilled like my assignments were unfinished. So, God propelled me into my purpose. Although life's disappointments made me want to shut down so many times, I was determined to try again this time with God, knowing I was anointed for whatever God had called me to plant, build, and birth.

God started teaching me how to embrace my authentic self. It was a challenge because I had to unlearn self-doubt, negative talk, and the belief system that I wasn't good enough. I started dressing up more and embracing the fashion side of myself, instead of dressing down to make people feel comfortable. Also, I am naturally a creator. God has graced me and has given the skills and knowledge to invent things without the education and experience. For example, I have known how to do hair since I was 13 years of age, and when I turned 16 I got even better.

God has taught me how to use my gifts to serve others. Not to sound like a cliché, but God can use you in every area of your life, not just in the church. I have had the pleasure of pouring into, encouraging, empowering, and equipping other women with the tools that God has placed in my hands. What I love the most is being able to build up women's self-esteem and self-worth with positive self-talk and makeovers. I encourage women to see themselves the way God sees them. I have done makeovers for battered women and women with self-esteem issues. I remember doing a makeover for a woman who cried afterwards because she didn't realize how beautiful she was. She had hidden herself for many years, hiding in her pain and the abuse she was experiencing. I encouraged her to find her voice and regain her power again. I know that every seed that God has allowed me to plant and sow in the lives of others is not in vain because shortly after, that woman got out of that abusive relationship and took baby steps toward seeking a relationship with God.

One day as I was driving, I heard clearly, "The spirit of Abigail." I asked God, "Lord what do you mean"? As soon as I parked, I began to pray and asked God for illumination. I then picked up my bible. God directed me to Abigail in the bible. I was in awe because of Abigail's character and her faithfulness and humbleness unto God. Although her husband was an evil man, she was yet a woman of prayer and character, and later on after the death of her husband she married David. After reading the scriptures, I realized that character is important and I must stay in position and be faithful to God no matter what opposition happens in my life. I was so encouraged and understood that God has a perfect plan no matter what it looks like. I understood that this narrow road of salvation isn't easy at all, and even when I fall short, God continues to show his love and kindness towards me. I realized that, not only am I called, but God has given me a unique purpose. God has increased my capacity to grow in every area of my life, removing men's limitations off my life. Also, God revealed the beauty and creativity that was in Abigail which I truly admire. God reminded me that I am graced with those same attributes.

Later while preparing for my wedding, I ran low on funds, and God reminded me to use my own creativity. So, I walked into the reception hall, looked around and came up with an all-pink reception theme that I decorated with the help and support of family members. I created a bouquet of roses, and gorgeous bling for each table. During the reception, I received so many compliments on how I decorated the place.

In 2017, by the leading of the Holy Spirit, I hosted my first prayer conference for my first women's ministry, Women Connects. The theme was "Power of a Praying Woman". I prayed and studied and made sure I prepared a manual for all the women who attended. The conference was effective. Deliverance happened in the conference. I then understood at the moment the importance of obeying God. Someone was waiting for me to show up in order to receive their breakthrough. With the support of the saints, the prayer warriors and one of my best friends, God had his way.

I remember a time when I shrank myself in certain environments instead of being who God called me to be. I was around envious and jealous people who were in my circle of influence and even in my family. I hid myself for a long time afraid to shine, flourish and blossom like a flower. Some people couldn't handle the essence of who God created me to be because of their own insecurities. The anointing on my life caused me to attract enemies. So, I shrunk myself to fit in places that I had outgrown. That place of comfort no longer had the capacity for me to grow. God himself was transitioning me to the next level. I was no longer graced in that place.

God has given me the power to dominate and conquer while on earth, and to use my gift to glorify him. God had to break me out of my comfort zones so that I could arise and do what he instructed me to do. I had to step into the unfamiliar, launch into the deep and build what God had placed in my hands to build. God was leading me to do some personal development so that I could grow beyond where I was to where God was taking me.

CHAPTER 41

Walking In My Purpose

FOR MANY YEARS I ALLOWED THE SPIRIT OF FEAR AND PROCRASTINATION to hinder me from excelling in life. I stayed stuck because of past life failures, disappointments and failed opportunities concerning business and life. I remember I would start a project, business, etc, and as soon as it didn't seem like it was working, I would get discouraged and quit. I would give up too soon, allowing fear to creep in while dealing with unbelief concerning what God had spoken to me. In prayer I would ask God to please help my unbelief. During my second year in college, God told me to start a gift basket business. I did what God said, but I needed to be rebuked because I said, "God, I'm not going to college to start a basket company," and I proceeded to laugh. I realized that my faith was small, not even understanding that my basket company could have been bigger than I could have imagined because God gave me the business idea.

With maturity, trial and error have taught me a lot. I realize that whatever God does is bigger than man's comprehension. Life has also taught me not to cage God in a box. The next business God gave me required a different version of myself and a level up mindset. God showed me that not only can he use people from the pulpit, but in corporate America, the marketplace, and on platforms. I had to learn that it does not matter what capacity God uses me in as long as I am humble and glorify and honor him in everything I do.

When I entered a new season in my life, God gave me a finishing anointing. God assured me, "Now is the time!" I could not allow opposition to deter me from my destiny. I had to learn that God has given me the power to dominate and conquer on earth what he has placed in my hands. Whether it was business, ministry, or any other facet of life, I had to approach it with assurance and confidence in God, first, knowing he has called, established and equipped me for the work. My gifts and talents were to glorify God first because God is the gift giver. There were talents inside of me and, whatever God was giving me to birth, it was my responsibility to carry it out. God was leading me to build platforms and walk in the momentum that he had given me. I was tired of being in the same predicament and staying in comfort zones too long. Now was my season to pivot and shift my mindset so I could become the woman that God has called me to be.

God has given me many platforms and ministries. My women's ministry was birthed in 2017. This was not just a typical ministry, but it was a God inspired ministry to help empower the whole woman. While some ministries focus just on spirituality, Women Connect focuses on building up women and encouraging them to identify their purpose in God and walk in the purpose. It encourages women to find their voice and rise from a dead place. At one point, I allowed people to validate this ministry, but God would not allow it to be controlled by people's perceptions, only by the Holy Spirit. When Women Connect was first birthed, I realized, like myself, that many women were in bondage and they wanted to be free in God. Some people were abused by spiritual leaders that they were under, and some just struggled from mental health issues, hurt and rejection. It was not my job to change them but to introduce them to a God that could deliver them. Many people sit in the church broken and wounded, and they need healing and extra support. My women's ministry created a sisterhood environment to help encourage all women, no matter the nationalities. My women's ministry came directly from God and I am grateful that God allowed it to be effective. Also, God has given me a business mentor group called Purpose Driven Women's Society on Facebook. The mission is to mentor business women, corporate America women, coaches, authors, and consultants. God has used me to help be a resource to someone that needs assistance in so many areas, like housing, finances, business, and much more.

I love to encourage the youth and speak life into them. I am partnering with some youth organizations to assist with mentorship programs. God continues to dwell within me, teaching me how to lead by guiding me the right way so I can help equip the next generation, or Generation X. God has also allowed me to use my platform in order to help first time or seasoned business owners have successful businesses. God birthed this book out of me because I wanted to take the time to share the important lessons I learned as a woman in the midst of all the trauma, pain, and rejection. I had to be rebuilt up as a woman. Before, I was particularly good at burying my problems and going on with life as normal. Sometimes a woman has to have a sabbatical and focus on the rebuilding up of herself as a woman. I realized that I do not always have to be so strong. There is a myth that says that black women have to be so strong. Oftentimes, we have been put in leadership roles as single parents, employees, career women, or just as women that do not have men to help contribute to our households.

I had the opportunity of seeing women in my family in leadership roles. In fact, I rarely saw my mother cry in front of her children. Being able to unwind and cry sometimes is important. I do not have to be strong all the time. I felt like a lot of my depression came from the mindset that "as a black woman, staying strong is what you do." I remember receiving a word from a spiritual sister who told me, "Release all of the burdens that you've been carrying. That's not what God intended for us to do. We are only vessels. You are not God." This word really resonated in my spirit. I didn't realize that I could be somebody's hindrance and not even know it. Sometimes you can want the best for people and give so much out of yourself that people become dead weight. I had to realize that some people move at different paces, and some do not want to grow in life. God had to show me the difference. At that moment, I realized that I needed to release some people.

I remember asking myself, "Why me?" I then responded to myself, "Why not me?" With maturity, I came to understand and learned how to ask the right questions. "God, what are you trying to teach me from this lesson?" And at that moment, my mindset shifted. I learned that complaining will not change the outcome of my life, but only intensify it. Sometimes you have to change your perspective on how you look at life. I started praying more and allowing God to illuminate his word to me. I started setting standards about who I was as a child of God, refusing to accept anything that does not image God.

CHAPTER 42

Walking In The Freedom Of The Lord

I F YOU HAVEN'T BEEN IN BONDAGE, HOW WOULD YOU KNOW WHAT freedom feels like? God was equipping me for the next level in him. I had to be tried, tested, and proven to bring glory and honor to God's name. God shaped me through my trials and showed his infinite power in my life. For many years, I allowed myself to stay stagnated in bondage with people and places to please people and to be accepted. People's perceptions of me were more important than what God said about me, not understanding that God was calling me from unhealthy connections and environments where my spirit was vexed. God had already validated and confirmed who I am in him. Oftentimes, there is always a battle going on in my mind of knowing who I am in Christ Jesus and walking in it.

You will never know what freedom is until you've been in bondage. I was in bondage to things that I thought were God, but they were really part of an unhealthy church culture that was suffocating me. God started revealing so much to me as a disciple. I realized that I needed a relationship with God, not religion. I realized that oftentimes in my past I was in churches and organizations that manipulated me for selfish gain. Sometimes they manipulated me for my money, my gifts, or simply for the church image. I realized at that time I wasn't growing. So, God himself illuminated his word to me concerning biblical truths. I had to unlearn those inserted man-made rules and viewpoints that weren't Biblical, even those within the traditions of my family.

I no longer needed man's approval to deem me worthy, once I realized that I was defined by God. Before, I struggled with an identity crisis, not knowing who I was in the kingdom of God. I allowed so many labels and curses to be spoken over my life by man. There is power in the tongue. Matter of fact, you can do so much damage with the tongue. You can manifest things in the atmosphere with what you speak out of your mouth.

I know that God has blessed me with so many gifts not only to be used in the kingdom of God, but to possess the land given me. God has graced me to be prosperous in business, creativity, and impacting and enriching the lives of other people. Many years I would minimize my gifts and hide them so the people that labored among me would not kill the vision that God had given me. I was afraid to blossom because of fear of the enemies snatching the vision if exposed prematurely. However, I learned to unapologetically be me and embrace who I am even if I did not live up to men's expectations. Oftentimes men put expectations on you that aren't approved by God. I have to choose Jesus Christ over the crowd. I have to be willing to obey God over man even if they are not in agreement with the call that is placed on my life. Many years ago, God started dealing with me about the control and manipulation families, leadership, and religious organizations had over the people of God. God showed me at the time that he wasn't in it. In fact, a lot of people were suffering in silence because of the abuse coming from the people of God. I remember one day getting it. So, I now just have a goal to please my father and focus on his agenda. There is freedom in serving God when you allow the Holy Spirit to lead you.

CHAPTER 43

Divine Elevations Divine Accelerations

FOR MANY YEARS, I WAS THE WOMAN WHO SAT ON THE SIDELINES AND watched my peers win in their endeavors. Some of those wins occurred because God placed me in the position to help others birth businesses, books, and much more. I told my dreams to people that had man-power and knowledge to help assist me in my vision. But with all of my pouring out and being their personal cheerleader, it actually caused friction with some. I realized that there wasn't any reciprocity, and I became drained, frustrated and discouraged. Although I was doing it from the heart, with the skills, personal development, and education, in reality, I was acting as a business and a mindset coach and didn't even know it. In fact, I have always had a grace for business, and in 2010, I received my associates degree in Business Administration & Management. I was now living my purpose by helping someone else achieve their goals. However, God saw the hearts of the people that I was helping and told me to set healthy business boundaries. After dealing with the wrong business connections, God showed me that I have to discern my connections.

As a boutique owner, doing relaunches can be good for business exposure and brands. One summer my business was doing well, and I wanted a completely different look. I wanted to see something different. I wanted a tailor-made boutique. I reached out to a woman in the marketing business who was also a believer. She completely did the opposite of what I asked for. She wasn't professional and my business was under construction for at least six months. I did not make any money from my online customers. I was so frustrated and angry, and I continued to reach out to her company to find out what was going on. I was told I was going to get a full refund, but it didn't happen. I was upset, but I realized that I had to pray and continue to seek God on when to reopen my online store. As I began to pray God gave me all new strategies and ideas. I learned a lesson from this situation and had to completely forgive the company for the wrong that was done to me and move forward. God showed me that my connections matter. People from different states started reaching out to me to see how they could assist me in my business. Some were coaches, consultants, and authors. Some coaches offered their services for free. Those new connections were valuable.

Sometimes you don't really know who you are and the powerful gifts and inspiration that God placed inside of you. God literally put people in my life to help pull those gifts out of me and nurture and assist me in my business journey. I never imagined in a million years that I would be in the position to show up as the highest version of myself. God surrounded me with people of high caliber and entrepreneurs who were on assignment to help women, like myself, to identify their purposes in life. I remember after losing a family member, my coach friend noticed that I wasn't on social media as much. This woman of God reached out to me and prayed and poured into me. All I remember doing is weeping and I felt my strength come back. I told her how much I appreciated her, and shortly after, it was back to business, knowing that life has to go on. God connected me with like-minded people. But I was also shown how important it is to be rooted and grounded in God's word and the wealth principles of sowing and reaping. Even though these ladies were making 5, 6, and 7 figures, they realized none of this was possible without God. I started investing more in myself and staying faithful to the vision God had placed in me.

I have always had the vision to encourage, empower, educate and build up people so that they can excel in life. God wants us to prosper and be in good health even as our souls prosper. For years I started doing research and self-educating myself on investments, homeownership, and valuable growth development information that was going to help people go to the next level in life. I realized that a lot of people are stuck in cycles and poverty mindsets because of a lack of knowledge or resources. God started placing it on my heart to release the resources for free. There were so many coaches that were telling me to charge for my services and make it into a business, but my focus was to obey what God instructed me to do. God has graced me in the area to help build a community where they are able to thrive in life. There is a generation of people that lack the necessary step-by-step information for starting a business. The bible says that "People perish for lack of knowledge." I realized that God is in control of my destiny. I could not be an influential woman without the Holy Spirit that dwells in me. God knew me when I was in my mother's womb. I always knew I was going to work in the fashion industry, but I never thought I would be a motivational speaker. Even as a boutique owner there are women, as well as men, that come up to me and ask me to coach them on their startup business. Some people witnessed first-hand my business journey and saw the trial and error and the growth of my business.

Family is essential. I am big on family. I was blessed to birth three children of my own, but God blessed me with more children that are not in my blood-line, but are very dear to my heart. God took my bad and turned it around for my good. I encourage people that are going through a life full of trauma, hurt, pain, and rejection to understand that God has the power to change your bad around for your good. You can live a life of restoration. Your past does not have to determine your destiny. God is the author and finisher of your faith. I realize how every experience in my life helped shape me into the woman that I am today. Without a test there is no testimony.

CHAPTER 44

Speaking Up About Sexual Abuse

EVEN THOUGH IT HAD BEEN SEVERAL YEARS SINCE I HAD EXPERIENCED sexual abuse, God allowed me to use my voice to speak up about it. I said to myself, "My voice will be heard. I will no longer muzzle my mouth. No means no!" I am the voice for the voiceless and an advocate for people who are in fear of telling their stories. I spoke on a platform to bring awareness to this form of abuse. God allowed me to tell my testimony and shed light on sexual abuse and how God helped me heal and forgive my violator.

I realized that getting sexually abused in my early teenage years was not only for me but for many other people after me that have been sexually abused. I encouraged other women or men to speak up about it, instead of internalizing that pain, which was not good for their mental health. There are people who were molested as children and are still dealing with those childhood wounds because they did not have the chance to heal. God used me to talk to other people about molestation and rape and to encourage them to get some counseling, healing, and deliverance for being sexually abused. Oftentimes people who have been rape or molested struggle with self-esteem issues and accept all kinds of abuse from people, thinking it's love. Some of my female and male cousins have been speaking out about sexual abuse that they experienced as children and as young adults. Speaking up about sexual and physical abuse is not a popular topic but it is important to talk about.

I am a voice for the people that had to experience this painful journey and had their mouths muzzled for fear of speaking up. Opening up about molestation, rape, and abuse can be the beginning of the journey of healing. So, I encourage men, women, teens and children to speak up about sexual abuse. Also, it's so important for parents to pay attention to the signs when babies are getting abused because babies can't speak up for themselves.

It's important to confront this painful reality and take back your power. There are so many people that have been molested as children and are still dealing with those childhood wounds that they did not heal from. God used me to talk to other people about molestation and rape and to encourage them to get some counseling or healing for being sexually abused.

Even males are getting the courage to speak up about their sexual abuse from people in ministry. Oftentimes men have a hard time expressing how they feel or talking about this topic because it makes them shameful or embarrassed about the sexual abuse. Some males go through the healing process and spend time in God's presence for deliverance. I always emphasize that it's not my fault neither is it their fault or anyone who was a victim of sexual and physical abuse. No means no, and it's not okay for this behavior to be justified.

There are so many untold stories of sexual abuse in my own family. I've watched family members suffer in silence. I always encourage those family members to speak out about it. It's important to seek some form of counseling for it. Being in the African American culture, family means everything from good food, music, family traditions, and also secrets. I realize that many parents grew up in a different era where the black family needed to stay together. Meanwhile in someone's home, a child is suffering because someone that is close to them is molesting them. When I was sexually abused, I had the same fear that a lot of people that are abused feel. But I am grateful to God that I had a mother fighting for me and supporting me all the way.

I am a sexual abuse survivor. I began to glean off of other healed victims. I began talking to a woman that was extremely close to me. She survived sexual abuse several times and yet was able to show up healthy in society. She opened up about her horrific experience of being violated multiple times. She felt like she wasn't going to make it out alive. Once God kept her, she later was, not only a living testimony, but a survivor. From her I learned that although this form of abuse does not disappear, it does not have to destroy your life. I had to learn how to be patient with my healing process and understand my healing process would not look like others, and it did not matter as long as I healed. After releasing the hurt and pain, at that point I started living a healthy lifestyle, a normal life without fear, knowing my future was secure in God. Hearing her testimony helped me change my perspective on releasing the pain and forgiving so that I could move on. It changed the narrative of my life and I started living a purposeful God-filled life.

Sexual abuse affected everything: my identity, relationships, image and confidence. But confronting this past experience has allowed me to regain a clear focus on my purpose in life. I no longer feel discarded and filthy, but I am whole and valuable as a woman. I know that I am enough and wonderfully and fearfully made.

CHAPTER 45

Finding My True Identity In God

IT WAS HARD DISCOVERING MY PURPOSE AND UNDERSTANDING MY identity in Christ. My past experience of the sexual abuse as a teenager made it almost impossible for me to see purpose beyond my pain. For many years I identified myself by the abuse that happened to me when I was younger, which made it hard for me to see myself the way God sees me.

For many years as a child and, even in my adulthood, I had to denounce false labels that were placed on me by people, and declare the word of God over my life. Even though God had revealed who I was in him, somehow, I allowed man's voice to become louder than God's. God had to remind me of a time when he revealed that I have an evangelist ministry and a prophetic calling on my life. The problem was that I was in church environments where they saw the giftings, but weren't willing to help groom and bring out the gifts.

I began to lose sight of who I was in God. Brokenness had me blinded without clarity of my divine purpose. I knew I had a calling on my life, but I ran for years because of feelings of unworthiness. My mother, who is an evangelist and a watchman, helped, mentored, covered, and groomed me as a young woman growing in God. As my mother sought God for guidance in her walk with him, she also sought God for clarity of who her children were in the kingdom of God. To this day she still actively mentors and encourages me to walk confidently in the things of the Lord. As a young woman growing up in ministry, I witnessed my mom's boldness. She preached the word of the Lord in different churches. I witnessed the power of God and true transformation through God's word. I was reminded that

I am chosen by God to do his will. I continued to get confirmation of what God had already spoken. I was oftentimes misunderstood, but eventually God sent people outside the four walls who handled me with love and care to confirm what God had already spoken.

I had to experience jealousy from people who used me for their gain. God revealed to me groups that secretly gossiped about me. But the truth of the matter is that their labels weren't who God created me to be. Some labels that were placed on me were contrary to God's voice. It was very important to me to know who I was to God and in God and to walk in my divine purpose concerning God's will for my life. There were so many roles and titles that were placed on me in church and in my everyday life. Sometimes there was confusion when I started operating in an area that God had not graced me in.

Growing up, going to church was very important to me and it was a part of my lifestyle. From going to school 5 days a week to having church service at least 3-4 days a week, fellowshipping with the saints was a major part of the era I grew up in. I began to ask God in secret, "Lord who am I? What do you see in me that I don't see? Lord, I want to identify you in me." God brought back to my remembrance when he revealed to me at 16 years old that I had an Evangelistic ministry inside of me. But for many years, I was lost in men's identity of who they thought I was, and fell when I allowed their opinions to become valid and prominent in my life.

God sent me reminders from dreams and prophetic utterances. One day I went to a women's ministry fellowship, and the service was really high. Prayer and worship set the atmosphere. There was a woman of God who asked me to pray for her. The prayer was like a refilling because she prophesied, prayed, and encouraged others. As I prayed, she began to pray for me and told me, "Do what God called you to do no matter what. And what they called you is not who you are. God has called you higher." At that moment I remembered the gifts that God placed in me: Evangelistic ministry, intercession and prophetic dreams.

I realized that God had given me a prophetic gift. I was a dreamer and God had used me to prophesy several times not even understanding it at the time. I left my grandma's church when I was a young lady, so I never got the proper teaching concerning my gifts. Oftentimes people knew that I was a seer and abused my gift. I would always second guess what I was feeling and discerning in the spirit. Then one day God showed me that what I was feeling was true, but how I responded was important. I grew up in a prophetic household, and all my siblings have prophetic gifts. All my children have prophetic gifts. My son has visions and will know things before they happen. My middle daughter is a seer and can see clearly, and my youngest child is a dreamer. My daughter's dad can also see clearly. So, when my children speak of things that they see or hear I listen to them.

After being broken and mishandled from abusive leadership, God had to teach me how to protect my children in their giftings. I had to cover my children from false labels, slander and carnal conversations and teach them how to love in spite of what they see in people. Also, I taught them to have compassion and pray for people no matter what.

In 2020, I prayed and asked God to allow me to see clearly because somehow, along my life's journey, my vision became blurry. Before, I could write a book of dreams and how they came to pass, and God would allow me to prophesy to people without fully understanding the gift. Growing up with this gift was heavy because I never wanted to wear what I saw on my face. I would be in the presence of people that God showed me things about. When I was young it was hard to look at them differently. The older I got, the more I matured in my walk and gifts. God taught me how to pray for what he showed me and not allow my emotions to control what God had called me to do.

God told me to increase my devotional time with him by reading the word of God and praying. Prayer can shift situations and atmospheres. God heightened my discernment and I was able to see things clearly. I learned not to override what the Holy Spirit was showing me. I fell short because of the way I responded to chaos. I learned that I have to give myself grace. I realized as a young woman I had a zeal and a love for God but the enemy sent people, even in the church, to sabotage me and hinder me from growing in God. The numerous attacks against my family and myself led to me not practicing self-control.

As children in the kingdom, we don't celebrate the fall of a brother or a sister, but we help lift them up in prayer. God began to open my eyes to the things that were not of him and to expose the spiritual wickedness that was going on. I've learned that anything or any atmosphere that is controlling is witchcraft. I understand that God does not want his children in bondage but to be free to serve him. Anything that does not represent the kingdom of God is a place that I have to remove myself from. I realize in my past I was abused, controlled, manipulated, and in bondage. The whole time I felt I was called to be loyal to man while not pleasing God. If your loyalty causes you to go against God then removing yourself from the situation or bucking against anyone is not sin. If God is not in it, then I cannot stay. I continue to pray and ask God to show me myself and also the hearts of people connected to me.

I had to go through a pruning and trimming process to kill off any dead and unproductive fruit that was rooted in me, and whatever hindered me from growing in God. God began to peel off the old man. I had to be tried, persecuted, rejected, and deal with many life oppositions for the call. I had to stand and see the salvation of the Lord. I had to go through to become the woman that God has called me to be today. I am glad about it because I stood firm on the word of God.

I am so grateful for the spiritual maturity. Yes, betrayal hurts and being mishandled hurts, but God and time heal wounds. The same people that have tried to break me, I can now smile at them and not hold on to what they have done because I gave it to God and released it. God made every plot and plan that the enemy had against my purpose and destiny fail. Being under the right covering has helped me grow and develop into who God created me to be.

CHAPTER 46

God Rebuilding My Character

FOR YEARS I WAS SO BIG ON MAINTAINING A RESPECTABLE REPUTATION. I went above and beyond to try to protect my name, not even realizing that people will talk about you whether you're doing good or bad. This comes with the territory of being a believer. Several times I was lied on and betrayed. I found out later that my reputation was people's perceptions about me. However, it was my character that was important to God. God had to deal with the old nature in me. Once I gave my life to Christ, what I did prior was forgiven and remembered no more. As I continued to grow in my walk, God taught me the importance of my character mirroring his image.

As a believer who was raised in the church, dying daily was a very important key element to living a righteous life. There were moments of my life where I struggled with my old man. Sometimes I was dealing with confrontation. I was definitely a peacemaker, but oftentimes I did not set up healthy boundaries. There were times that I gravitated to my old nature, what I knew and was exposed to as a child. Some things got to me and shook me. I wondered about the motives of the people who were connected to me. Were they for me or against me?

In 2019, God really revealed where I was in my faith walk and that there was still room for growth. I prayed and asked God to show me and he did. The truth sometimes hurts. I learned not to ask God for something that I am not prepared to receive. This lesson taught me where to seat people in my life. I also learned that I have to love myself enough not to force connections and to walk away from anyone that hinders me from growing, no matter who it is.

I did not want to confuse the people who are connected to my history with the people who are connected to my destiny. Every experience in my life helped shape me into being the woman that I am today. Without a test there is no testimony. I was dealing with friends that took advantage of my friendship. One thing I learned about me is that if I say I love you, I mean it. I do not take it lightly. I also learned that the enemy will always allow your good to be evil spoken of. I was tired of being connected to dysfunctional people. I realized I attracted a lot of broken people on my life's journey. I prayed that God would connect me to people that add value to my life, no more leeches. I realized that I did not value myself and allowed myself to be used for conversations, monetary gifts and much more. I was so misunderstood as a person, and I felt oftentimes that people would misinterpret what I was communicating. I was so comfortable with being an introvert that oftentimes people would think that I thought I was better. I wanted to be around people that understood my heart and knew that my intentions were good towards them. I had to deal with grown folks acting in an immature way because, somewhere along the way, they misunderstood the information that I communicated to them at the time. So, I realized forgiveness and not holding on to offenses were important. Once I learned how to love myself, I could forgive some people without continuing to put up with their toxic behaviors.

Respect in friendships is just as important as it is in relationships. Oftentimes, you have to teach people how to treat you. A good lesson to learn is not to allow hurt people to destroy your spirit and to know who is assigned to you. Not everyone should have access to you. Sometimes people treat you by how they were conditioned. I used to wonder why I endured so much warfare. It was because I allowed too many in my camp. Not everyone had pure intentions. I remember crying a lot about some of the rejection and ill intent that I saw with some of my friendships. My prayer was for God to show me who was seasonal and who was connected to my destiny. God showed me. The enemy was using someone that I loved to come up against me. I asked God to teach me how to get over people and to be okay with not being liked and being the center of secret conversations. I was shown but became unbothered. I realized God was fighting for me no matter what. The more the enemy fought against me, the more God blessed me right in the face of my enemy.

CHAPTER 47

Chosen

FROM THE MOMENT I WAS IN MY MOTHER'S WOMB I WAS CHOSEN, BUT oftentimes misunderstood. Growing up, misunderstandings caused a major fear of connecting with others. I always felt like I was an outcast because I was different. As a child, I remember asking God, "What's wrong with me? Why do I think different, look at life different from my immediate family?" Quite often I would get persecuted for not being like-minded. My talks about success bothered people. I remember as a little girl the eyes rolling and the irritated looks that were on people's faces when I talked. People would inflict their insecurities on me. I was told that I thought I was better than others, but I couldn't help having high dreams of being different and wanting a better life. The talks of business and goals were looked down on by people who thought differently than I did. Because I was different it caused me to be rejected by family and friends.

In spite of my painful memories of rejection, abandonment, not having the sense of belonging, and feeling overlooked and undervalued, God was hiding me until his perfect timing. Yet and still, I had a lot to say. God gave me a voice to speak truth and to spare not. For many years my voice was muzzled. Oftentimes God was downloading godly wisdom so that I wouldn't operate from a place of carnality. However, I wasn't walking in my truth and owning who God created me to be. Because of a lack of confidence and fear of rejection, oftentimes I was silent. In spite of my flaws, the spirit of boldness started to ooze out of me. I was left with no excuses. I was called on a great commission by God to spread the gospel and not compromise. I began to speak up about biblical principles. I stood with the broken and withdrew myself from prideful men.

Forgiveness should not just be preached or taught, but applied to our everyday lives. God was showing me believers who were walking in pride and no accountability. My spirit became vexed and I began to pray that God would not correct my love language, but correct those around me. God reminded me that there was room for my gift in the kingdom. Mathew 9:37 says, "Then saith he unto his disciples, the harvest is plentiful, but the laborers are few." I realized that there is so much to do in the kingdom of God. I have a divine purpose and God has invested in me what I need in order to be effective in the ministries that he placed in me. In 2017 God gave me a women's ministry, a powerful influential platform to teach biblical truths, empower, equip, encourage, and share powerful resources. I realized that oftentimes communities and church bodies are missing out on women ministries. Women ministries should not just be a social club or a place for fellowship, but a place for a complete transformation. God wanted me to target the whole woman, so as women, we can be fulfilled in God.

I finally got it. I started to see what God saw in me, an intercessor and trailblazer for the kingdom of God. I surrendered my life unto my Lord and Savior with no more compromising in order to fit in and be accepted. I realized I am enough and equipped to do God's will. I began to rise up out of the ashes and had the audacity to show up in every space that God created me to be in, no longer feeling like I was an imposter, but knowing I am a part of the royal family.

God created me to occupy every space that I was in. I began to cancel every voice of the enemy concerning my purpose. There were moments when the enemy tried to talk me out of giving birth. But I wasn't aborting in that season. I was giving birth. I began to love myself naked, embrace the real me and accept my authentic uniqueness. God blessed me with gifts and talents and I was going to use them no matter who was not in agreement with it. God reminded me not to call what is uncommon ungodly. However, I struggled with some of my assignments. Sometimes I obeyed and sometimes I didn't. So, God would always send confirmation that I was on the right track. Oftentimes I was in God's will, and when I wasn't, I was reminded to do what God called me to do, to step outside my comfort zone and obey God. Last year, I was at a women's conference and a Prophetess told me, "What they are calling you is not who you are. God has called you higher." Although I wanted to hide on the sidelines, I knew she was in the vein because of what God revealed when I took a sabbatical. During my sabbatical, I was healing from sickness and for family reasons, but God was speaking to me clearly. Since I could rely on no one but God during this time, God began to reveal so much to me. He reminded me that time was at hand and now was the time to walk confidently in my calling. I gave God my yes completely and came in alignment with his will, seeking his perfect will for my life.

CHAPTER 48

From Pain To Purpose

NO AMOUNT OF PAIN OR TURBULENCE CAN DETER ME FROM MY destiny. My trials and tribulations have not been wasted, but they were necessary for my making. It's working for my good. God had to shift my whole mindset and make me realize my purpose belongs to him. My life does not belong to me. I was bought with a price.

I realized I had to relieve myself from past disappointments, doubt and the fear of failure that were deeply rooted inside of me. My behavior mirrored what was inside of me. The pain, doubt, rejection, and lack of confidence hindered me from progressing in life. I was walking in unbelief. I felt like I didn't deserve to be loved and accepted because of past experiences. Oftentimes, I would self-sabotage because I felt unworthy to do God's will. I allowed my limited beliefs to keep me in the same predicament for years.

I was in an on-going cycle going around the same mountain. I kept trying to do it my way instead of doing it God's way and staying rooted and grounded in his word in every season of my life. Life had a way of making me release my own control and allow God to be in complete control of my life. I completely became vulnerable and transparent to God telling him where I was and allowing him to heal my heart and my mind. My pain served a purpose. God rescued and restored me when I was without purpose, living in sin.

God had placed so many gifts and talents inside me, and I had to be reminded of all the things that I placed on the shelf because of my own fear, doubt, and insecurities. God was calling those gifts forward. I would have vivid dreams of God taking me to a higher level in him. There was a greater level of power and authority that I was purposed to walk in.

I was also reminded me of painful moments in my life when I experienced many losses. I had to relieve myself from my past. So, I tried to measure and control every move as if I was able to keep myself. I started to rely on the bag instead of God. I was afraid of dealing with the grief of losing again. God had to change my whole mindset so that I could be a good steward over what he had given me. Whatever God gives me, I must give to God first, and God will maintain it.

I remember asking God to change my situation, but instead God changed me in my situation. Maturity in God allowed me to look at life differently and understand that it was time to grab a hold of the vision that God had placed inside of me. Once I started to line up with what God told me, everything around me started to line up, including ministry, family, business, and my personal women's ministry. I was no longer guilty of disobeying God. I was now walking in abundance, not because I deserved it, but because it was my birthright in Christ.

The pain is what helped birth my promise. God, who is beyond my comprehension, is not limited by man's ability. Therefore, I have given God free reign over my life to be used by him as a vessel to bring his word. God showed me a dream of me ministering to women in schools and coliseums, encouraging them to rise, walk in their purpose and go after their dreams. God has sent me many confirmations concerning the dream he showed me. So, I will do what God says do even if people walk out of my life. God gets the glory out of my life. I realize the enemy was not after how pretty I thought I was, but he was after my oil, the anointing that was on my life. He tried to keep me frustrated and burnt out so that I would not accomplish my divine purpose. However, the crushing, abandonment, betrayal, rumors, and rejection were necessary, because they positioned me where God wanted me to be. I am no longer a foreigner, but a servant of Christ.

I repented and fully surrendered to the will of God even though it felt uncomfortable. I then saw the favor of God so heavy on my life. Blessings were chasing me down. I began to possess my promised land. Because I obeyed God by sowing seed on good soil, I was blessed with free dinners and bills paid in full with zero balances. I was receiving blessings and promotions that, in the natural, I was not qualified for. I was in God's will. I was not perfect, but God had justified me. I told God that, no matter how he blessed me, I wanted to stay in a kneeled down position. I no longer allowed fear to dictate my future, but I kept trusting the God that is in control of my future.

I remember when God told me at church to make room for the newness. God was expanding my territory, and I was grateful. I no longer just talked about walking in purpose because God himself was allowing me to walk in purpose. God gave me dominion over my land. My language changed and my faith was elevated. So many people looked at me like I was crazy, but I didn't care. I was no longer going to kill the vision with my words. Instead I was staying in position to receive my blessings and not feel guilty for walking in the favor of the Lord. A divine elevation took place once I released the steering wheel and allowed God to be in control of my life completely!

One of my main priorities is taking care of my home. My first ministry is home with my family building a strong foundation inside of the home and learning how to have a healthy balance in life. I continue to teach love and biblical teachings in the home. Oftentimes it's hard as a married woman to wear so many hats understanding the enemy's target is family. However, by the grace of God his strength continues to keep me going, and prayer has been a powerful tool that keeps me in communication with God.

My greatest passion is working with teens and young adults. God has graced me in that area to continue to teach, encourage and love on them. I realize that the teens are at the mercy of their parents and society, and my job is teaching them biblical truths and showing them that they can rise from any painful dysfunction or prodigal son or daughter situation and still be used by God.

My businesses are flourishing and I am impacting my tribe that God has called me to. God has given me a platform of influence to draw people to him. Never in a million years would I have thought that the little insecure girl, who was always in the background, would now be the woman with a voice that is needed in the earth. Now I am the woman, who is invited by people with major platforms, to speak a word of encouragement and tell my testimony.

After much preparation by God, I set out to accomplish what God called me to do. Obedience and prayer became my posture. I wasn't concerned about how others felt about what God was calling me to do. I was no longer the woman I used to be. I was broken at the feet of Jesus to find my identity and purpose in God. In my brokenness is where I encountered God. God taught me how to love myself and to not lean on my own might for strength but God's strength. Even in difficult times I learned not to trust my own emotions, or others' opinions of me.

I am someone's survival guide. There are people that are depending on me to show up and do what God has called me to do. No, I am not perfect, but I have been forgiven and restored. I am following the leading of the Holy Spirit, knowing that God's will will be done in my life. God has anointed me to preach the gospel, write books, and be a Christian entrepreneur in the marketplace.

At the age of 23, a prophet told me that God wanted me to tell my story and that some people would be so surprised about the things I've been through. I wasn't ready because I was still dealing with old wounds and past life traumas. Years later during a pandemic when the whole world was in a place of unfamiliarity, God inspired me to write my life story again. I had the nerve to obey God and write my story. While it was not easy to open up about my past life, it helped me to face my past, which was hindering my future. I am on a road of healing and recovery and being whole in Christ Jesus.

I realized that there is beauty in pain. I had to stay the course because it was working for my good. Romans 8:28 (NIV) says, "And we know that in all things God works for the good of those who love him, who have been called according to his purpose." When God told me this time to write my story, it was different. God was not only allowing me to birth my life story, but to help someone to understand that they can come from the hardest places in their life and still be used for the glory of God. I am someone's survival guide and all the glory goes to Jesus Christ.

Where God currently has me serving is preparing me for where God is taking me. I am in training and learning how to remain faithful to God and show up in ministries God has called me to. God is maturing and developing my gifts to use for his glory and shifting me to another dimension in him. I am not a survivor, but I am a conquer. With the power of God, I now conquer the very thing that tried to destroy me. It's under my feet. I am converted, a new woman in God, standing on the word of God and allowing God to be my anchor.

CHAPTER 49

Reintroducing Myself

I DON'T LOOK LIKE WHAT I'VE BEEN THROUGH BECAUSE GOD HAS KEPT me when I couldn't keep myself. He lifted my head when I couldn't hold my head up. I am glad that I stayed with God even in the midst of my trials. I am a living witness that God will keep and restore you because he did it for me.

I am in my now season. Promotion and favor are overtaking my life because it's God ordained. Sometimes, with growth, it seemed like I was breaking, but God was preparing and positioning me for his will.

There is a new season of opportunities and open doors that only God purposed for my life. God has given me a finishing anointing, so that I can finish what God has placed in my hands to build. This is God's appointed time for me to go forth in all God has anointed me to do. There is a supernatural acceleration that is happening in my life quickly. I am trusting God with the unknown, launching out into the deep, moving into an unfamiliar place. God is enlarging my tent beyond my comprehension.

When I aligned myself with the word of God everything started to flourish. God replaced the wrong people in my life with divine connections and destiny helpers. I wanted to be connected to people who celebrated me, not just tolerated me. God placed leaders in my life who trained me and activated me for the work of the Lord. Some of those connections were people I met through mutual connections, conferences, and Christian platforms.

God connected me with powerful women and men of God who were pastors, authors, coaches, and consultants who supported the vision that God gave me and encouraged me to continue in the things of God.

God reminded me that I needed to obey and be active in my women's ministry that he had given me. I was called to the broken, wounded, hopeless, discarded, and rejected people. I had to be willing to obey God and be willing to lose the crowd. I had a choice to make and obedience was my choice.

I started to travel for ministry and business. I made business friends in different states, and I began working on building and networking with other business owners. God gave me entrepreneurial grace. I remember being the one that was lost completely concerning business. There were people who were business gurus who wouldn't extend help. God allowed me to experience this treatment and called me to be different. God downloaded in me strategies to continue to inspire, equip, and empower women on my platform and in business. Now, I am not so caught up in people's opinions of me, but I am living the life that my father ordained for me to live.

There were Christian entrepreneurs that were sent to me to help me unlock my potential. I was just obeying God's voice breaking generational poverty and barriers and creating generational wealth. God allowed me to use my God-given talents to do what I was called to do in the earth. God has called me to conquer, prosper, and evolve in all facets of life. There's no limit to what God can do in my life.

I realize the power lies in me knowing who I am in God and the power of God that is within me. I understand who I am in the spirit. God reminded me there is more, not only what God requires of me, but there is more that God has in store for me. I am walking in more and in my purpose. I took a leap of faith and trusted God's perfect plan and perfect timing. I am in my purpose and walking in the abundance of God's favor.

Despite the business frustrations, God has given me more witty ideas, vision, and provision. I started out with one co-author project. Now I have other book projects, and I am collaborating with more authors around the world. I am now a business, transformational, and life coach. Who would have thought a girl with a speech impediment would be booked for speaking engagements and mentoring men and women to walk in more of what God has for them.

I am unapologetically flourishing into the woman that God called me to be. I've been tested, tried, and proven to do his will. Even in the midst of healing from the spirit of rejection, God put his stamp of approval on me. God has elevated me and has given me the grace to finish my assignments, do ministry, and give birth to every vision and gifting that is placed inside of me. I am in my purpose walking into the new version of who God created me to be.

ABOUT THE AUTHOR

Hi, my name is Author Love. I was born and raised in Cincinnati, Ohio to my mother Constance and my father Man. I was raised in a single-family home with my mother and three other siblings. I am the oldest of my mother's children. My father wasn't present in my life growing up. I was raised and active in ministry since I was young.

I believe I was about 14 years old when I realized there was greatness inside me. At that age, I knew that God had given me the gift of exhorting and influencing. As a teen parent, I had my first speaking engagement and my confidence increased. Also, I saw the major impact I had on my audience.

I had a great passion for helping people. Later, I went through medical training and got my CNA certification. I worked in the medical field for 18 years of my life and also worked in several leadership positions. I have worked with the youth since the age of 18 as a mentor in school settings as well as in ministries.

At 26 years of age, I graduated from college in 2010 and obtained an associate degree in business administration and management.

I am the founder and CEO of several women ministries on Facebook. God's mission for my women's ministry is to build up the total woman mentally, physically, spiritually, and financially, and to encourage them to identify what their purpose is and walk in it, while God illuminates to them the power that lies within.

I am a Co-Author of a powerful prayer book called *121 Days of Prayer* and *Mental Health Matters Book*.

Printed in the United States
by Baker & Taylor Publisher Services